WALKING IN THE FOOTPRINTS OF CHRIST JESUS

A Christ-Centered Workshop to a Positive Mental Wellness

Christopher Willis

PublishAmerica
Baltimore

Softcover 9781627091282
PUBLISHED BY PUBLISHAMERICA, LLLP
www.publishamerica.com
Baltimore

Printed in the United States of America

Table of Contents

The Lord's Prayer

Our Father,
who art in heaven,
hallowed is thy name.
Thy Kingdom come,
thy will be done,
on earth as it is in heaven
Give us this day our daily bread.
And forgive us our trespasses,
as we forgive those who trespass against us.
And lead us not into temptation,
but deliver us from evil.
For thine is the kingdom,
The power and the glory,
Forever and ever.
Amen.

The Serenity Prayer

God grant me the serenity
to accept the things I cannot change;
courage to change the things I can;
and wisdom to know the difference.
Living one day at a time;
Enjoying one moment at a time;
Accepting hardships as the pathway to peace;
Taking, as He did, this sinful world
as it is, not as I would have it;
Trusting that He will make all things right
if I surrender to His Will;
That I may be reasonably happy in this life
and supremely happy with Him
Forever in the next.
Amen.

Connect all nine dots by using four lines and not picking up the pencil from the paper.

Anger

Matthew 5:21-26

[21] "You have heard that it was said to the people long ago, 'You shall not murder, and anyone who murders will be subject to judgment.' [22] But I tell you that anyone who is angry with a brother or sister will be subject to judgment. Again, anyone who says to a brother or sister, 'Raca, is answerable to the court. And anyone who says, 'You fool!' will be in danger of the fire of hell.

[23] "Therefore, if you are offering your gift at the altar and there remember that your brother or sister has something against you, [24] leave your gift there in front of the altar. First go and be reconciled to them; then come and offer your gift.

[25] "Settle matters quickly with your adversary who is taking you to court. Do it while you are still together on the way, or your adversary may hand you over to the judge, and the judge may hand you over to the officer, and you may be thrown into prison. [26] Truly I tell you, you will not get out until you have paid the last penny.

Ephesians 4:26-27. "In your anger do not sin: Do not let the sun go down while you are still angry, and do not give the devil a foothold"

Introduction Workshop Series Goal: To increase your understanding of the different pathways involved in managing problems and issues through information, discussion and experiential exercises. You will gain insight and develop skills on effective and appropriate communication of anger.

Connect all nine dots by using four lines and not picking up the pencil from the paper.

Overview: Anger as an Emotion
Anger as a Physiological Response Anger as a Thought Process Anger Management through Interpersonal Training Confidentiality (in and out of group) (15 min.)
Develop group rules which include:
Treat all group members with respect
Don't hurt anyone else or yourself
No physical aggression
No judgments, be supportive of others
Be aware of language

Anger Management Emotion Group Check In Defining-Emotion Brainstorm and write on board definition of emotion Discuss how emotions are a form of communication.

Perceptions of Anger A. How is anger viewed in our society?

Present the idea that anger is just an emotion that's been judged or perceived in a certain way; it is generally thought of as negative and something to avoid at whatever cost. One way to understand anger differently is to challenge some of our perceptions. Hand out Misconception about Emotions, Hidden Anger & Identifying Feelings. Facilitate a discussion to include the following topics: Now did mom do mad? Now did dad do mad? HOW did other significant people do mad? What was the response when you got mad? Do you find that you currently do any of these things?

1. Psycho-education content: Function/Purpose of anger: message or indicator we send to ourselves that we're not happy. Need to know what to do with that message. Appropriate and inappropriate ways of dealing with anger. Point of workshop is to learn alternatives to communication and expressions of anger. Process responses and reactions to handout Regulating Emotions (15 minutes)

Emotional

- **Body Biofeedback:** By discovering the way your body feels when anger is approaching, you can use that feeling as a cue for altering your physiological response or altering your thoughts and behavior so your anger does not get out of hand.
- **Generating Alternative Arousal:** Using anger as a cue to generate an alternative form of physical arousal that is antagonistic to anger or arousal (i.e. relaxation & humor)
- **Channeling Arousal-** Using the arousal you acquire from being angry as a powerful source of energy that helps you handle a provocative situation.

Communication

- **Assertiveness** - Teach you to stand up for your legitimate rights and express your needs in an appropriate way.
- **Listening** –allows you to open up communication channels.
- **Negotiation-** process by which two people work the conflict out by coming to a mutually satisfying agreement
- **Criticism** - the ability to give and receive constructive criticism.
- **Confrontation** - the ability to take responsibility for perceiving a situation or a person's behavior as unacceptable. Once identified, specifically describe the unacceptable behavior or situation. Stating clearly the tangible effects of the event.
- **Praise** – decreases the chances of the other person becoming defensive

Feelings
   A. Feeling awareness - prior to expressing feelings in a productive way. It is necessary to acknowledge they exist.
   B. Expressing feelings - ability to express feelings in positive ways.
   C. Making positive affect work for you - keep yourself in a positive mood, induce positive affect in others, find everyday uppers{no drugs), offer help whenever you can, and be kind.

Behavior
Present the idea that the goal of emotion regulation is not to get rid of emotions, but to increase our awareness of them. Present the idea that intense emotions have powerful immediate and after effects on our memory, thoughts, behavior, and interpersonal relationships. Thus it is important to learn how to manage and regulate our emotions.
   • First step in regulating emotions is identifying feelings. Accurately label feelings (look at sheet for types of emotions). Determine magnitude of feels (look at the level of intensity of emotion- high-low).
   • Increase awareness of facial expressions & body changes.
   • Be mindful. Define; small shifts in our awareness; becoming aware of our own experience, and state mind. Mindfulness is being more aware of what we are experiencing in our mind and body from moment to moment.
   • Understanding Hidden Anger Present idea of proportionate and disproportionate responses to situations. (stimulus-response model) Discuss how residual (left-over) anger may be the result

of previously unresolved situations, leading to "Hidden Anger", other causes for hidden anger may include: Unrealistic expectations. Physical, emotional abuse Exposure to violence or abuse Greater sensitivity to stress

• Self- soothing Exercise Introduce deep-breathing as one technique for regulating emotions and managing hidden anger.

Psychology of Anger

Anger is a natural and mostly automatic response to pain of one form or another (physical or emotional). Anger can occur when people don't feel well, feel rejected, feel threatened, or experience some loss. The type of pain does not matter; the important thing is that the pain experienced is unpleasant. Because anger never occurs in isolation but rather is necessarily preceded by pain feelings, it is often characterized as a 'secondhand' emotion.

Pain alone is not enough to cause anger. Anger occurs when pain is combined with some anger-triggering thought. Thoughts that can trigger anger include personal assessments, assumptions, evaluations, or interpretations of situations that makes people think that someone else is attempting (consciously or not) to hurt them. In this sense, anger is a social emotion. You always have a target that your anger is directed toward (even if that target is yourself). Feelings of pain, combined with anger-triggering thoughts motivate you to take action, face threats and defend yourself by striking out toward the target you think is causing you pain.

A Substitute Emotion

Anger can also be a substitute emotion. By this we mean that sometimes people make themselves angry so that they don't have to feel pain. People change their feelings of pain into anger because it feels better to be angry than it does to be in pain. This changing of pain into anger may be done consciously or unconsciously.

Being angry rather than simply in pain has a number of advantages, primarily among them distraction. People in pain generally think about their pain. However, angry people think about harming those who have caused pain. Part of the transmutation of pain into anger involves an attention shift – from self-focus to other-focus. Anger thus temporarily protects people from having to recognize and deal with their painful real feelings; you get to worry about getting back at the people you're angry with instead. Making yourself angry can help you to hide the reality that you find a situation frightening or that you feel vulnerable.

In addition to providing a good smoke screen for feelings of vulnerability, becoming angry also creates a feeling of righteousness, power and moral superiority that is not present when someone is merely in pain. When you are angry, you are angry with cause. "The people who have hurt me are wrong – they should be punished" is the common refrain. It is very rare that someone will get angry with someone they do not think has harmed them in some significant fashion.

The definition of whether someone's anger is a problem often turns on whether or not other people agree with them that their anger, and the actions they take in the name of their anger, is justified. Angry people most always feel that their anger is justified. However, other people don't always agree. The social judgment of anger creates real consequences for the angry person. An angry person may feel justified in committing an angry, aggressive action, but if a judge or jury of peers does not see it that way, that angry person may go to jail. If a boss doesn't agree that anger expressed towards a customer is justified, a job may be lost. If a spouse doesn't agree that anger was justified, a marriage may have problems.

Whether justified or unjustified, the seductive feeling of righteousness associated with anger offers a powerful temporary boost to self-esteem. It is more satisfying to feel angry than to acknowledge the painful feelings associated with vulnerability. You can use anger to convert feelings of vulnerability and helplessness into feelings of control and power. Some people develop an unconscious habit of transforming almost all of their vulnerable feelings into anger so they can avoid having to deal with them. The problem becomes that even when anger distracts you from the fact that you feel vulnerable, you still at some level feel vulnerable. Anger cannot make pain disappear – it only distracts you from it. Anger generally does not resolve or address the problems that made you feel fearful or vulnerable in the first place, and it can create new problems, including social and health issues.

What is Anger?

Anger is a basic human emotion that is experienced by all people. Typically triggered by an emotional hurt, anger is usually experienced as an unpleasant feeling that occurs when we think we have been injured, mistreated, opposed in our long-held views, or when we are faced with obstacles that keep us from attaining personal goals.

The experience of anger varies widely; how often anger occurs, how intensely it is felt, and how long it lasts are different for each person. People also vary in how easily they get angry (their anger threshold), as well as how comfortable they are with feeling angry. Some people are always getting angry while others seldom feel angry. Some people are very aware of their anger, while others fail to recognize anger when it occurs. Some experts suggest that the average adult gets angry about once a day and annoyed or peeved about three times a day. Other anger management experts suggest that getting angry fifteen times a day is more likely a realistic average. Regardless of how often we actually experience anger, it is a common and unavoidable emotion.

Anger can be constructive or destructive. When well managed, anger or annoyance has very few detrimental health or interpersonal consequences. At its roots, anger is a signal to you that something in your environment isn't right. It captures your attention and motivates you to take action to correct that wrong thing. How you end up handling the anger signal has very important consequences for your overall health and welfare, however. When you express anger, your actions trigger others to become defensive and angry too. Blood pressure rises and stress hormones flow. Violence can ensue. You may develop a reputation as a dangerous 'loose cannon' whom no one wants to be around.

Out of control anger alienates friends, co-workers and family members. It also has a clear relationship with health problems and early mortality. Hostile, aggressive anger not only increases your risk for an early death, but also your risk for social isolation, which itself is a major risk factor for serious illness and death. These are but two of many reasons why learning to properly manage anger is a good idea.

Anger Styles Are Learned

Although everyone experiences anger in response to frustrating or abusive situations, most anger is generally short-lived. No one is born with a chronic anger problem. Rather, chronic anger and aggressive response styles are learned.

There are multiple ways that people learn an aggressive angry expression style. Some people learn to be angry in childhood by copying the behavior of angry people around them who influence others by being hostile and making threats. For instance, children growing up in a household where one parent constantly berates and belittles the other learn to berate and belittle themselves, and then often recreate this behavior when they grow up and enter into relationships by berating and belittling their partners. Someone who has learned to act in an angry way may not realize that they have an anger problem. From their perspective, they are just acting 'normally' (e.g., meaning normal for their family of origin).

Anger victims' desire for revenge or mastery can also cause them to develop anger problems. An abused child may vow at some level to never again let him or herself be vulnerable, and start himself becoming hostile towards others on the theory that "a good offense is the best defense". Alternatively, abused or wounded people may over generalize and seek revenge against an entire group of people, only some of whom may have actually harmed them. As an illustration of this revenge principle, consider the sometimes aggressive prejudiced responses that some Americans experience towards immigrants who come from countries that were once United States enemies; Japanese, and Vietnamese people, for example, or persons subscribing to the Islamic faith today.

Still another way people can learn to be aggressively hostile involves their being reinforced and rewarded for being a bully. People who bully someone once and then find others respecting or fearing them more for their aggressive actions become quite motivated to continue bullying. Bullies go on to use aggression more and more because they find that it helps raise their social status and position.

Recognizing Anger Signs

Before you learn the techniques to manage your emotions, you first need to learn to recognize your anger. You need answers to questions like:

- "How do I know when I am angry?"
- "What events/people/places/things make me angry?"
- "How do I react when I'm angry?"
- "How does my angry reaction affect others?"

Answering these questions takes a while. It is likely you can rattle off several things that make you angry. You might even be able to identify several signs that you exhibit when you are angry (e.g., clenched fists, etc.). These quick answers are only the beginning, however; the low hanging fruit. You will want to continually ask yourself these questions for a period of time before you can be satisfied that you are fully knowledgeable about your personal anger.

Recognizing Physiological Signs of Anger

The first step in effective anger management is to learn how to recognize when you are angry. Some angry people see their emotions as a black or white state—they are either raging mad or they are calm. In reality, anger is not black and white, but rather quite gray. Anger occurs on a continuum between rage and calm where most of the time people experience some gradation of anger between these two extremes.

The same people who tend to see anger in terms of extremes sometimes have difficulty recognizing when they are experiencing intermediate anger states. Luckily, most people experience a number of physical, emotional and behavioral cues that they can use to let them know when they are becoming upset.

Some physical signs of anger include:
- clenching your jaws or grinding your teeth
- headache
- stomach ache
- increased and rapid heart rate
- sweating, especially your palms
- feeling hot in the neck/face
- shaking or trembling
- dizziness

Emotionally you may feel:
- like you want to get away from the situation
- irritated
- sad or depressed
- guilty
- resentful
- anxious
- like striking out verbally or physically

Also, you may notice that you are:
- rubbing your head
- cupping your fist with your other hand
- pacing
- getting sarcastic

- losing your sense of humor
- acting in an abusive or abrasive manner
- craving a drink, a smoke or other substances that relax you
- raising your voice
- beginning to yell, scream, or cry

Relaxation Techniques

The following discussion describes common anger management techniques. These techniques will not produce results if you use them only casually—you must be committed to actually using and practicing these techniques before they can have any chance of positively affecting your life.

Controlled Deep Breathing and Muscle Relaxation

Your breathing rate and heart rate both increase when you become emotionally aroused. You can learn to reverse these increases by deliberately slowing your breathing and/or systematically relaxing your tense muscles. Relaxing in this manner will help you to maintain control.

You may find yourself breathing quick, shallow breaths when you are upset. Allowing this shallow chest-only breathing to continue will only exacerbate your anger. Instead, take action to redirect your breathing and relax your muscles so that you will calm down. Set aside at least 15 minutes in which to do this exercise. Less time than this will not likely be beneficial!

Start your relaxation efforts by taking several slow and deep breaths in a row, each time taking care to exhale for twice as long as you inhale. Count slowly to four as you breathe in, and then breathe out slowly as you count to eight. As you do this, notice where the air in your lungs is going. Open your lungs and breath deeply across the lung's full range. Your breath should enter your belly first, then your chest, and finally your upper chest just below your shoulders. Feel your ribs expand as your lungs expand. Pay attention to how your ribs return to their original location as you exhale completely. Continue this breathing pattern for several minutes, returning immediately to normal breathing if at any time you feel odd or out of breath.

The Anger System - for anger workout and emotional release

Tools for Coping with Life's Stressors

As you progress in your recovery from the behavioral consequences of low self-esteem, you will need to deal with the powerful emotion of anger. It is important to use all of these tools during your recovery process. It is important to recognize the course of the anger cycle so you can use an ANGER workout system to escape this cycle.

The typical unhealthy anger cycle is:

When you express anger in your old "sick" way, the automatic natural response is guilt for hurting the feelings of the person. You immediately feel remorse. You then suppress the anger. However, you still feel resentment over the real or perceived stimulus which prompted your anger. If you are again irritated by this or a similar stimuli, you will express anger again. It is not useful in your recovery process to express your anger directly on people in the old ``sick" way which keeps you trapped in the anger cycle. For this reason, use the ANGER workout system when you get angry.

- A - Accept
- N - Name
- G - Get It Out
- E - Energize
- R - Resume

A - Accept

First, you need to accept that what you are feeling is anger. There is often a tendency to deny this powerful emotion because your experience with anger in the past has been painful, hurtful, or disastrous. Don't deny your anger. Face it head on for what it is.

N - Name

Second, you need to name and identify what is getting you so angry. You need to name what it is about the stimulus which is triggering your response. Utilize alert system to help you to analyze and think out what is going on to get you angry. You need to identify not only the current anger but also the old unresolved anger that the stimulus may be provoking.

G - Get It Out

Third, you now need to get it out of your system by expressive emotional release of anger workout. Get yourself in a private place (if you can) to use one of the following activities to aggressively ventilate you anger on inanimate objects rather than on people:

- Yelling in your head silently
- Yelling in a car with windows closed
- Yelling in a room away from others
- Yelling into a paper bag or pillow
- Beating on pillows, cushions, or mattress
- Hitting a punching bag, weight bag
- Screaming in a vacant field or lot
- Screaming with a towel in your mouth
- Ripping a telephone book, newspaper, or catalogue

E - Energize

Fourth, once you have aggressively ventilated and experienced emotional release of the anger, you will energize yourself to feel calmer, more relaxed, less anxious, less tense, or less stressed. Aggressive anger work will enable you to be more rational and realistic and better able to use the alert systems to promote your recovery.

R - Resume

Fifth, once you are energized, resume your involvement with the person who was the stimulus of the anger and assertively confront the person with how you feel in a calm, cool, rational manner.

Checklist for Hidden Anger

If we have any national fault it is hiding our own anger from ourselves. Here is a checklist to help you determine if you are hiding your anger from yourself. Any of these is usually a sign of hidden anger.

• Procrastination in the completion of imposed tasks.
• Perpetual or habitual lateness.
• Sarcasm, cynicism, or flippancy in conversation.
• Over-politeness, constant cheerfulness, attitude of "grin and bear".
• Frequent sighing.
• Smiling while hurting or feeling angry.
• Frequent disturbing or frightening dreams.
• Over-controlled monotone speaking voice.
• Difficulty in getting to sleep or sleeping through the night.

• Boredom, apathy, loss of interest in things you are usually enthusiastic about.
• Slowing down of movement; feeling lethargic.
• Getting tired more easily than usual.
• Excessive irritability.
• Getting drowsy at inappropriate times.
• Sleeping more than usual.
• Waking up tired rather than rested and refreshed.
• Clenched jaws - especially while sleeping.
• Facial tics, fist clenching, and similar repeated physical acts done unintentionally or unaware
• Grinding of the teeth - especially while sleeping.
• Chronically stiff or sore neck.
• Chronic depression- extended periods of feeling down for no reason. This is not about rage. This is about the feelings we call " irritation", "annoyance", or "getting mad" We are taught to avoid expressing these feelings and to avoid having them If possible.
• Learning our anger actions- identify the behaviors we do when we are angry through: modeling, operant learning, de-escalating anger (time-out) and creative time out.
• Generating productive angry behaviors - prevent anger from escalating and rid yourself of anger actions.
• Changing your behavior: making new actions easier - replacing negative responses to anger with new more positive behaviors.
• Learn the ABC's of anger - this method helps you to establish what caused you to be angry (Anger trigger), what you did about it {Behavior), and what happened because of what you did (Consequence).

Unfortunately, many people go overboard in controlling negative feelings; they not only control their expression, but their awareness of them, too.

Because you are unaware of being angry does not mean you are not angry. It is the anger you are unaware of which can do the most damage to you and to your relationships with other people, since it does get expressed, but in inappropriate ways. Freud once likened anger to the smoke in an old-fashioned wood-burning stove. The normal avenue for discharge of the smoke is up the chimney; if the normal avenue is blocked, the smoke will leak out of the stove in unintended ways - around the door, through the grates, etc. -chocking everyone in the room. If all avenues of escape are blocked the fire goes out and the stove ceases to function. Likewise, the natural expression of anger can be blocked, just like a chimney; this blockage can be disruptive to yourself and others. Our expression can be stifled in an effort to protect ourselves, by continually suppressing our feelings that we are not angry, even when we are. Such self deception is seldom completely successful, and the blocked anger "leaks out" in inappropriate ways, some of which are previously listed. The items in the list are all "danger signals" that negative feelings are being bottled up inside. It is true that each of them have causes other than anger (procrastination for example, can be due to an unreasonable fear of failure), but the presence of any of them is reason enough for you to look within yourself for buried resentments. If you are human, you will find some. If you are fortunate, you will find few, since you will have learned effective ways of discharging them. If you are like most of us, you will have to unlearn some old habits before you can learn new ways handling these feelings - ways that are constructive rather than destructive. Getting rid of a lifetime accumulation of buried resentments is a major task, which is one of the goats of counseling. Whether such a process is necessary for you is best decided in consultation with a qualified professional person.

Anger Inventory

While we were still Children, many of us made choices about the way we were (or were not) going to relate to our feelings. These early decisions may still be shaping your emotional life today. Answer the following questions about your childhood experiences with anger. If you didn't grow-up with a mother and/or a father, substitute the name of someone who took care of you when you were growing up.

When my mother got angry, she?

When my father got angry, he?

When _____(another household or family member) got angry, he/she?

When I got angry (as a child), I?

Based on my experiences growing up, I think the following about anger?

Now, when I get angry, I?

Now, when someone else gets angry with me, I?

Misconceptions about Emotions

1. There is a right way to feel in every situation.
Reality challenge:

2. Letting others know that I am feeling bad is a weakness.
Reality challenge/;

3. Feeling angry is bad and destructive.
Reality challenge:

4. Being emotional means being out-of-control.
Reality challenge:

5. Emotions can just happen for no reason.
Reality challenge:

6. Some emotions are really stupid, a waste.
Reality challenge:

7. All painful emotions are a result of a bad attitude or a weak character.
Reality challenge:

8. If others don't approve of my feelings, I shouldn't feel that way.
Reality challenge:

9. Other people are the best judge of how I am feeling, not me.
Reality challenge:

10. Painful emotions should just be ignored.
Reality challenge:

11. Anger is a bad thing.
Reality challenge:

12. If I get angry, people won't like me anymore.
Reality challenge:

Depression

"The spirit of a man will sustain him in sickness, but who can bear a broken spirit?" (Proverbs 18:14)

"I am laid low in the dust; preserve my life according to your word" (Psalm 119:25).

"Trust in the LORD with all your heart, and lean not on your own understanding; in all your ways acknowledge Him, And He shall direct your paths." (Proverbs 3:5-6; NKJV)

"I am troubled, I am bowed down greatly; I go mourning all the day long. ...I groan because of the turmoil of my heart" (Psalm 38:6, 8 - NKJV).

Connect all nine dots by using four lines and not picking up the pencil from the paper.

Garden Your Mind: Recognize, Remove, Replace

"Hear counsel, and receive instruction, that thou mayest be wise in thy latter end."-- Proverbs 19:20 -

OBJECTIVE:

Learn to manage your thinking by relating the management of your thinking to the management of a garden.

MOTIVATION:

Wouldn't you agree that it would be nice to have a clear and easy way to understand how to improve your attitude? Don't you agree that by improving your attitude, you improve your life by improving at least your problem-solving and coping abilities?

GARDEN: The first thing that you must understand in order to be an effective gardener is the difference between weeds and plants. Else, how can you make good use of the soil? Therefore, the first principle is **RECOGNIZE.** If you cannot recognize the problem, you certainly cannot either problem-solve how to fix the problem or learn to cope effectively with the problem. Once you can recognize the difference between weeds and plants, then you need to remove the weeds. As any gardener can tell you, weeds steal the resources that your plants need and weeds will even choke out and kill your plants. Therefore, the second principle is **REMOVE.**

If you cannot remove the problem, you certainly cannot keep from having the problem over and over again. Once you have recognized and removed the weeds, you then need to replace the weeds with plants. There is not much point to having clean soil if you are not going to plant in it. The fact is, if you do not plant in the clean soil, then the weeds will find their way back into your soil. Therefore, the third principle is **REPLACE.**

If you do not replace the weeds with plants, then the weeds will gradually come back. The weeds are the self-defeating thoughts and scripts. The plants are the helpful and productive thoughts and scripts. The clean soil is the quiet and empty mind. The recognizing is the awareness of the short- and long-term results that your thinking provides: "Wherefore by their fruits ye shall know them."--Matthew 7:20. The removing is disputing or talking yourself out of the stinking thinking. The replacing is the planting and nurturing of practical, factual, logical, positive, problem-solving, coping, risk taking, etc., thinking that helps you to achieve your healthy goals. The replacing is making good use of your mind by devoting it to healthy and helpful thinking styles.

BRIEF SUMMARY: You need to **RECOGNIZE** the weeds in your mind, to **REMOVE** the weeds from your mind, and to **REPLACE** the weeds in your mind with productive plants. That is, recognize and remove your hurtful thinking and replace it with helpful thinking.

SELF AND GARDEN: You are the garden **NOT** the weeds or plants in the garden. You are the mind, **NOT** the weeds or plants in the mind. The weeds and plants come and go, but the garden remains constant. The weeds and plants grow, develop, and change, but the garden remains the same.

COPING WITH DEPRESSION It's Time to Find Your Key to Your Depression!

HELP RELAX YOUR DEPRESSION AWAY   Great Ways to De-Stress And Improve Your Mood

Your shoulders are tense, your back hurts. You feel grouchy and know it's all due to stress. What can you do? The relaxation techniques described below can help relieve both the physical and emotional tension and moodiness that often follows stressful situations. 1.Relax Your Body 2.Deep

Breathing 3.Stretching 4.Exercise 5.Take a bath 6.Get a massage 7.Eat Well 8.Relax Your Emotions 9.Relaxing your emotions can be just as important as relaxing your body in relieving depression. 10.Talk 11.Laugh 12.Cry 13. Read 14.Do something you love

CHANGE AND DEPRESSION

Change is a fact of life. In every dimension of our lives, the one thing we can count on is that "things will change". In some instances we initiate the change. In others it may be beyond our control. Regardless of how change happens, it will represent a shift from the expected. And this shift will require a period of adjustment. Life is altered in some way and we are confronted with new realities. While we respond to change as individuals, adjustment usually occurs in stages as we proceed through the change process. Change is a natural healing process that should not be blocked or interfered with. Change helps us to learn more about ourselves and our emotional makeup and our patterns of living. We are all changing different things and acknowledging our change helps us to move forward to new opportunities and experiences while not forsaking the past and what we have experienced and learned from it.

TIPS FOR COPING WITH DEPRESSION

Be in charge of your depression reactions (attitude). Modify your expectations and your reality. Be tolerant of any mistakes made by others involved. They are feeling the stress also. Expect stress; stay flexible and focus on coping today. Don't blame everything you don't like on the specific stressor itself or on others. Be prepared for "psychological soreness" and hurting at times. The soreness means that you are hurting and are healing. Use your depression as a personal opportunity for growth.

TIPS FOR BOOSTING YOURSELF-ESTEEM

Stay positive about yourself. Identify at least one good thing you have done everyday. Think of ways you overcame your depression. Surround yourself with other positive non-depressed people. Do not "buy into" useless criticism from others. Make selective decisions about whom you will accept suggestions from regarding changes or "improvements" you should make in yourself or in your life. Decreasing depression is to be focused on. Expect yourself to be responsible for yourself-esteem. If you don't initiate changes, nothing will ever change. Accept your weaknesses and mistakes you have made. Speak up for yourself, in an assertive (not aggressive) manner when it is important for you to do so. Take care of yourself. You have real needs which must be met before you can be effective doing anything else. Treat others with respect. This will add to the increasing self- esteem. Also, treat yourself with kindness and respect.

A TIME FOR EVERYTHING

In nature, with its laws and unchanging cycles, there is a time for everything, a wonderful and comforting predictability. While each of us may say we'd like Indian summer to last all the way through March, wouldn't our confidence in nature be a bit shaken if, just one year, nature decided to be "flexible", "hang loose, and veer from the schedule as originally planned? Depression is but a brief detour on the road of life. Keep your sense of humor. It helps to keep balance. Practice good stress management techniques. Design small projects that are successful. Keep doing your normal duties even if you are anxious. Talk about your depression with co-workers, family & friends. Acknowledge your feelings, take breaks and make a point of having fun even if you do not feel like it. Force yourself to go out.

SEVEN WAYS FOR YOU TO FIGHT BACK

1. **STAY HEALTHY** When your body is under stress, you need to eat right, get adequate rest and exercise, and keep a regular schedule. 2. **KNOW THE EFFECTS OF DEPRESSION** Know the sources of depression in your life. Pay close attention to your body and its stress signals. Correct them when possible. 3. **DON'T BLAME YOURSELF** Remember that too much depression is not personal failure. It is likely a situation caused by factors beyond your control. 4. **DON'T DEAL WITH THINGS ALONE** Let your friends, family and other people in the community help you get the information and help you need. 5. **DEVELOP SUPPORT SYSTEMS** The best way to fight grief is to talk with family and friends about what you are going through. 6. **HAVE A PLAN** Planning reduces coping with depression and gets things done. Have a plan for your day, week, your coping activities and for your future to minimize the likelihood of depression problems. 7. **STAY ACTIVE** Stay in touch with friends and co-workers and family members. Get out and go places. Learn something new. Volunteer your services. Start exercising when you can.

HOW TO BEAT THE DEPRESSION BLUES
Eight Depression Warning Signs

1. **GETTING SICK MORE OFTEN** Having more coughs, colds, flu, or stomach trouble, no energy, feeling tired all the time. 2. **NOT SLEEPING WELL AT NIGHT** Not being able to sleep. Sleeping more or during the day. 3. **USING MORE ALCOHOL OR DRUGS** Drinking or using drugs by yourself. Staying high all the time. Needing alcohol or drugs to get through the day. 4. **BECOMING MORE ISOLATED** Not wanting to see family or friends. Not going out. Staying home all the time. Isolating and ignoring requests to interact with others. *5* **LOSING INTEREST IN THINGS** Not wanting to do things you enjoy or work on projects you have started. Just wanting to "keep it simple" even though it is not. 6. **PUTTING THINGS OFF** Feeling there is plenty of time to get things done, but never getting around to them. Procrastination of daily simple activities. 7. **LONG PERIODS OF DEPRESSION** Feeling down, feeling unable to cope with problems. No energy to deal with anything. A lack of motivation. 8. **HAVING MORE FIGHTS WITH YOUR FAMILY** Getting upset over things that never use to bother you. Feeling angry and irritable more often than you used to.

Relaxation
Relaxation is the opposite of depression. Relaxation means that the mind and body are calm. As the mind and body remain in a calm state of reduced arousal, they become refreshed and restored. Although sleep is essential, even sleep is not pure relaxation. In sleep we alternate between periods of deep rest and dreams, our minds are extremely active. Emotionally

charged dreams or fretful sleep can cause us to wake up even more tired than when we went to sleep. Very effective restoring is done at an even keel, while awake. Although you may not reach the deepest level of rest possible in sleep, the fact that you can steadily remain at a level of reduced arousal can be more refreshing than sleep. It is hard to remain anxious when you are relaxed Try it. The aim of relaxation, then is to free yourself from your depression long enough to refresh and restore your mind and body. Relaxation only requires a few minutes once or twice a day, and an attitude of calm. BODY RELAXATION BREATHING DEEP MUSCLE RELAXATION PROGRESSIVE MUSCLE RELAXATION MIND RELAXATION IMAGERY

Depression Management

Problem Solving Tool Thinking Yourself Back to Reality Exercise:

A Way of Managing Disrupting and Interfering and Defocusing Thoughts

Thought or Feeling that I am having which is a problem: What is NOT true about my problematic thought or feeling? What's the worst thing that could happen in this situation? How likely is that to happen in this situation? How awful, is the worst thing that could possibly happen? How could I learn from this experience'? What thoughts and actions would help me cope with this situation? What can I do to counter doubt, anxiety and depressed thoughts/ feelings? What can I do not to repeat this problem situation again?

SELF-TALK CYCLE

The self-talk cycle is the constant conversation we have with ourselves about what is happening to us and around us. However, we don't store and record the 'truth" we store and record the "truth" as we see it. So if we decide to change or grow, this self-image becomes our major barrier to change. Then when we make mistakes, as we all do, we don't stop there. We continue to beat ourselves with our self-talk about the mistake, which makes that cycle even stronger next time!

Example: You have just been released from prison and you are going to a job interview. In your mind you are carrying on a conversation about how you have never been able to get and hold a job before. You think about all the people in prison who say it is impossible to get a good job with a record. By the time you get to the interview you have convinced yourself you can't get the job, so you do very poorly in the interview and. YOU DON'T GET THE JOB! As you leave the interview, you tell yourself how stupid it was to even go through the efforts of applying.

CAUTION
Our present thoughts determine our future...if we change the way we think we change the way we act!!!
We move toward what we think about, and we usually think about what we don't want!

This is one of the most important concepts we can understand as human beings. We all tend to focus on what we don't want. We think about the problem rather than the solution. Then just like the boy on the bike, we don't want to hit the rock, but we look at the rock. What do we hit? The rock!! Where are you spending time in your mind? Is yourself-talk leading you toward what you want in life, or toward the rocks?

List three areas where you are spending time in your mind concentrating on the problems instead of the solutions. Now are these areas challenges on you?

F   FALSE

E   EVIDENCE

A   APPEARING

R   REAL

Explore your fear. Where is it coming from? Channel that energy into action. When you have a clear plan and desire it is easier to work through your fear.

Make your desires clear. (Ask, Believe, Receive)
Ask for what you want.
- Conduct the "check up from the neck up" which is as follows:
- 1st Decide
- 2nd Focus
- 3rd Action

Believe
- Affirm yourself with your positive affirmations and positive self- talk.

• You will want to use your visualization aid and the power of your imagination.

Receive

• Become aware of what is going on around you. Keep your eyes open for opportunity.

Your brain doesn't know the truth from a lie. It believes whatever it is told. Make sure you tell it what you want your reality to become.

WHO AM I?

1. Who am I? (Qualities, characteristics, roles, etc)
2. What can I do?
3. What can't I do?
4. What do I believe I can do?
5. What do I believe I can't do?
6. What do I like most about myself?
7. What do I like least about myself?
8. When have I been really glad to be alive? What was I doing? Who was I with?
9. How much do I want to work?
10. What kind of reputation do I choose to have?

Anxiety

"Do not be anxious about anything, but in everything, by prayer and petition, with thanksgiving, present your requests to God. And the peace of God, which transcends all understanding, will guard your hearts and your minds in Christ Jesus" (Philippians 4:6-7).

"Humble yourselves, therefore, under God's mighty hand, that he may lift you up in due time. Cast all your anxiety on him because he cares for you" (1 Peter 5:6-7; Psalm 55:22-23)

"Then Jesus said to his disciples: 'Therefore I tell you, do not worry about your life, what you will eat; or about your body, what you will wear. Life is more than food, and the body more than clothes. Consider the ravens: They do not sow or reap, they have no storeroom or barn; yet God feeds them. And how much more valuable you are than birds! Who of you by worrying can add a single hour to his life? Since you cannot do this very little thing, why do you worry about the rest?'" (Luke 12:22-26, NIV; Matthew 6:25-34)

"Why are you downcast, O my soul? Why so disturbed within me? Put your hope in God, for I will yet praise him, my Savior and my God" (Psalm 42:5).

Connect all nine dots by using four lines and not picking up the pencil from the paper.

The word anxiety comes from the Latin word anxious, meaning a condition of agitation and distress. The term has been in use since the 1500s. Anxiety is one of the most misunderstood aspects of our daily living. It is often misdiagnosed and mistreated and can be overlooked for years in a person's life. You can better understand the nature of anxiety by looking both at what it is and what it and is not. For example, anxiety can be distinguished from fear in several ways. When you are afraid, your fear is usually directed toward some concrete, external object or situation. When you experience anxiety, on the other hand, you often can't specify what it is you're anxious about. The focus of anxiety is more internal to you than external or outside of you. It seems to be a response to a vague, distant, or even unrecognized danger. You might be anxious about "losing control" of yourself or some situation. Or you might feel a vague anxiety about "something bad happening." Anxiety affects your whole being It is a physiological, behavioral, and psychological reaction all at once. On a physiological level, anxiety may include bodily reactions such as rapid heartbeat, muscle tension, queasiness, dry mouth, or sweating. On a behavioral level, it can sabotage your ability to act, express yourself, or deal with certain everyday situations. Psychologically, anxiety is a subjective state of apprehension and uneasiness. In its most extreme form, it can cause you to feel detached from yourself and even fearful of dying or going crazy. The fact that anxiety can affect you on a physiological, behavioral, and psychological level has important implications for your attempts to recover. A complete program of recovery from an anxiety disorder must intervene at all three levels to 1. Reduce physiological reactivity 2. Avoidance behavior

3. Change your **Own** interpretations or "self-talk" to life events which perpetuate a state of apprehension and fear and worry in your life Anxiety can appear in different forms and at different levels of intensity. It can range in severity from a mere twinge of uneasiness to a full-blown panic attack marked by heart palpitations, disorientation, and terror. Anxiety that is not connected with any particular situation, that conies "out of the blue," is called free-floating anxiety or, in more severe instances, a spontaneous panic attack. The difference between an episode of free-floating anxiety and a spontaneous panic attack can be defined by whether you experience four or more of the following symptoms at the same time (the occurrence of four or more of the following symptoms defines a panic attack): Shortness of breath Heart palpitations (rapid or irregular heartbeat) Trembling or shaking Sweating Choking Nausea or abdominal distress Numbness Dizziness or unsteadiness Feeling of detachment or being out of touch with yourself Hot flashes or chills Fear of dying Fear of going crazy or out of control If your anxiety arises only in response to a specific situation, it is called situational anxiety or phobic anxiety Situational 0 anxiety is different from everyday fear in that **it** tends to be out of proportion or unrealistic. If you have a disproportionate apprehension about on freeways or confronting your spouse, this may qualify as situational anxiety. Situational anxiety becomes phobic when you actually start to avoid the situation: if you give up driving on freeways, going to doctors, or confronting your spouse altogether. In other words, phobic anxiety is situational anxiety that includes persistent avoidance of the situation. Often anxiety can be brought on merely by thinking about a particular situation. When you feel distressed about what might happen when or if you have to face one of

your phobic situations, you are experiencing what is called anticipatory anxiety. In its milder forms, anticipatory anxiety is indistinguishable from ordinary "worrying." But sometimes anticipatory anxiety becomes intense enough to be called anticipatory panic. There is an important difference between spontaneous anxiety (or panic) and anticipatory anxiety (or panic). Spontaneous anxiety tends to come out of the blue, peaks to a high level very rapidly, and then subsides gradually. The peak is usually reached within five minutes, followed by a gradual tapering-off period of an hour or more. Anticipatory anxiety, on the other hand, tends to build up more gradually in response to encountering-or simply thinking about-a threatening situation, and then usually falls off quickly. You may "worry yourself into frenzy" about something for an hour or more and then let go of the worry as you find something else to occupy your mind.

I) Long- term, Predisposing Causes A Heredity B. Childhood Circumstances 1. Your Parents Communicate an Overly Cautious View of the World 2. Your Parents Are Overly Critical and Set Excessively High Standards 3. Emotional Insecurity and Dependence 4. Your Parents Suppress Yourself-Assertiveness C. Cumulative Stress Over Time **II. Biological Causes** A. Physiology of Panic B. Panic Attacks and the Noradrenergic Hypothesis C. Generalized Anxiety and the GABA/Benzodiazepine Hypothesis D. Obsessive-Compulsive Disorder and the Serotonin W Hypothesis D. Medical Conditions That Can Cause Panic Attacks or Anxiety **III. Short-Term, Triggering Causes** A. Stressors That Precipitate Panic Attacks 1. Significant Personal Loss 2. Significant Life Change 3. Stimulants and Recreational Drugs B. Conditioning and the Origin of Phobias C. Trauma, Simple Phobias, and Post-Traumatic Stress Disorder **IV. Maintaining Causes**

A. Avoidance of phobic Situations B. Anxious Self-Talk C. Mistaken Beliefs D. Withheld Feelings E. Lack of Assertiveness F. Lack of Self-Nurturing Skills G. Muscle Tension H. Stimulants and Other Dietary Factors I. High-Stress Lifestyle J. Lack of Meaning or Sense of Purpose You will note that there are numerous contributors to anxiety which currently are known. You may not ever know the exact cause of your anxiety but it is very likely that there are several causes of your anxiety difficulties. Fear of losing control Fear of not being able to cope Fear of failure Fear of rejection or abandonment Fear of death and disease

Signs, Symptoms, Causes, and Effects

Learn to recognize stress symptoms and identify the situations that cause them. When these symptoms persist, you are at risk for serious health problems, because stress can exhaust your immune system.

What is stress?

Life can be stressful. We all face different challenges and obstacles, and sometimes the pressure is hard to handle. When we feel overwhelmed, under the gun, or unsure of how to meet the demands placed on us, we experience stress. In small doses, stress can be a good thing. It can give you the push you need, motivating you to do your best and to stay focused and alert. Stress is what keeps you on your toes during a presentation at work or drives you to study for your midterm when you'd rather be watching TV. But when the going gets too tough and life's demands exceed your ability to cope, stress becomes a threat to both your physical and emotional well-being.

Stress is a psychological and physiological response to events that upset our personal balance in some way. These events or demands are known as stressors. We usually think of stressors as being negative, such as an exhausting work schedule or a rocky relationship. However, anything that forces us to adjust can be a stressor. This includes positive events such as getting married or receiving a promotion. Regardless of whether an event is good or bad, if the changes it brings strain our coping skills and adaptive resources, the end result is the subjective feeling of stress and the body's biological stress response. According to the American Psychological Association, fifty-four percent of Americans are concerned about the level of stress in their everyday lives.

What causes stress and its symptoms?

The potential causes of stress are numerous. Your stress may be linked to outside factors such as the state of the world, the environment in which you live or work, or your family. Your stress can also come from your own irresponsible behavior, negative attitudes and feelings, or unrealistic expectations.

Furthermore, the causes of stress are highly individual. What you consider stressful depends on many factors, including your personality, general outlook on life, problem-solving abilities, and social support system. Something that's stressful to you may be neutral or even enjoyable to someone else. For example, your morning commute may make you anxious and tense because you worry that traffic will make you late. Others, however, may find the trip relaxing because they allow more than enough time and enjoy playing music or listening to books while they drive.

Stressors can be divided into three broad categories:

- Frustrations – Frustrations are obstacles that prevent you from meeting your needs or achieving personal goals. They can be external—such as discrimination, an unsatisfying job, divorce, or the death of a loved one—or internal. Examples of internal frustrations include physical handicaps, the lack of a desired ability or trait, and other real or perceived personal limitations.

- Conflicts – Stressors involving two or more incompatible needs or goals are known as conflicts. For example, a working mother might feel torn over a job offer that would advance her career, but take time away from her family. Sometimes the conflict involves a choice between two desirable options, such as deciding between two acceptance offers from equally appealing colleges. At other times, the decision involves disagreeable alternatives.
- Pressures – Stress can stem from the expectations of others or the demands you place on yourself. You may feel pressure to get good grades in order to please your parents or get into a good school. Or you may feel pressure to excel at work, make a difference in your community, or be the perfect mother.

Whether or not the source of stress causes significant emotional and physical symptoms depends in part on the nature of the stressor itself. Stressors that involve central aspects of your life or that persist for extended periods of time are more likely to result in severe distress and disruption of functioning. Furthermore, the more stressful situations or life changes you're dealing with at one time, the more intense the symptoms of stress.

What are the signs and symptoms of stress?

Stress affects the mind, body, and behavior in many ways. The specific signs and symptoms of stress vary from person to person, but all have the potential to harm your health, emotional well-being, and relationships with others. Below is a partial list of stress signs and symptoms that a person undergoing stress might experience.

Signs and Symptoms of Stress

Intellectual symptoms: How stress can affect your mind

Emotional symptoms: How stress can make you feel

- Memory problems.
- Difficulty making decisions.
- Inability to concentrate.
- Confusion.
- Seeing only the negative.
- Repetitive or racing thoughts.
- Poor judgment.
- Loss of objectivity.
- Desire to escape or run away.
- Moody and hypersensitive.
- Restlessness and anxiety.
- Depression.
- Anger and resentment.
- Easily irritated and "on edge".
- Sense of being overwhelmed.
- Lack of confidence.
- Apathy.
- Urge to laugh or cry at inappropriate times.

Physical symptoms: How stress can affect your body
Behavioral symptoms: How stress can affect your behavior
• Headaches.
• Digestive problems.
• Muscle tension and pain.
• Sleep disturbances.
• Fatigue.
• Chest pain, irregular heartbeat.
• High blood pressure.
• Weight gain or loss.
• Asthma or shortness of breath.
• Skin problems.
• Decreased sex drive.
• Eating more or less.
• Sleeping too much or too little.
• Isolating yourself from others.
• Neglecting your responsibilities.
• Increasing alcohol and drug use.
• Nervous habits (e.g. nail biting, pacing).
• Teeth grinding or jaw clenching.
• Overdoing activities such as exercising or shopping.
• Losing your temper.
• Overreacting to unexpected problems.

Keep in mind that the signs and symptoms of stress can be caused by other psychological or physical problems, so it's important that you consult a doctor to evaluate physical symptoms. Similarly, emotional symptoms such as anxiety or depression can mask conditions other than stress. It's important to find out whether or not they are stress-related.

What are the different types of stress?

Acute stress

Acute stress is the most common and most recognizable form of stress, the kind of sudden jolt in which you know exactly why you're stressed: you were just in a car accident; the school nurse just called; a bear just ambled onto your campsite. Or it can be something scary but thrilling, such as a parachute jump. Along with obvious dangers and threats, common causes of acute stressors include noise, isolation, crowding, and hunger. Normally, your body rests when these types of stressful events cease and your life gets back to normal. Because the effects are short-term, acute stress usually doesn't cause severe or permanent damage to the body.

Episodic acute Stress

Some people endure acute stress frequently; their lives are chaotic, out of control, and they always seem to be facing multiple stressful situations. They're always in a rush, always late, always taking on too many projects, handling too many demands. Unlike people for whom stress is a once-in-a-while spike, these folks are experiencing **episodic acute stress.**

According to the American Psychological Association, those prone to episodic acute stress include driven, hard-charging "Type A" personality types and worrywarts, always anxious about the next disaster they're sure lurks around the corner. While the Type A tends to seem angry and hostile and the worrier more depressed, both are frequently over-aroused and tense, and both are susceptible to the physical manifestations of extended stress, including high blood pressure and heart disease.

If you're prone to episodic acute stress, you may not know it or admit to it. You may be wedded to a life style that promotes stress. You may explain your frequent stress as temporary "I just have a million things going on right now", as integral to your work or home life "Things are always crazy around here", or as a part of your personality "I have a lot of nervous energy, that's all". You may blame your frequent stress on other people or outside events, or you might view it as entirely normal and unexceptional. Unfortunately, people with episodic acute stress may find it so habitual that they resist changing their lifestyles until they suffer severe physical symptoms.

Chronic stress

The APA Help Center describes **chronic stress** as "unrelenting demands and pressures for seemingly interminable periods of time." Chronic stress is stress that wears you down day after day and year after year, with no visible escape. It grinds away at both mental and physical health, leading to breakdown and even death. **Common causes of chronic stress include:**
- Poverty and financial worries
- Long-term unemployment
- Dysfunctional family relationships
- Caring for a chronically ill family member
- Feeling trapped in unhealthy relationships or career choices
- Living in an area besieged by war or violence
- Bullying or harassment
- Perfectionism

One of the most dangerous aspects of chronic stress is that people who suffer from it get used to it. They accept chronic stress as their lot in life, or they forget it's there. Because chronic stress is based on long-term, often intractable situations, both the mental and physical symptoms of chronic stress can be difficult to treat.

Traumatic stress
Severe stress reactions can result from a catastrophic event or intense experience such as a natural disaster, sexual assault, life-threatening accident, or participation in combat. After the initial shock and emotional fallout, many trauma victims gradually begin to recover. But for some people, the psychological and physical symptoms triggered by the trauma don't go away, the body doesn't regain its equilibrium, and life doesn't return to normal. This is a condition known as post-traumatic stress disorder (PTSD). Common symptoms include flashbacks or nightmares about the trauma, avoidance of places and things associated with the trauma, hyper vigilance for signs of danger, chronic irritability and tension, and depression. PTSD is a serious disorder that requires professional intervention.

What are the long-term effects of stress?

The stress response of the body is meant to protect and support us. When faced with a threat, whether it be to our physical safety or emotional equilibrium, the body's defenses kick into high gear in a process known as the "fight or flight" response. The sympathetic nervous system pumps out adrenaline, preparing us for emergency action. Our heart rate and blood flow to the large muscles increase, the blood vessels under the skin constrict to prevent blood loss in case of injury, the pupils dilate so we can see better, and our blood sugar ramps up, giving us an energy boost.

The stress response is what helped our stone age ancestors survive, enhancing their ability to fight or flee from danger. But in the modern world, most stressors are psychological, rather than physical. Caring for a chronically-ill child or getting audited by the IRS qualifies as stressful situations, but neither calls for either fight or flight. Unfortunately, our bodies don't make this distinction. Like a caveman confronting a saber tooth tiger, we go into automatic overdrive, releasing the same hormones that enabled prehistoric humans to move and think faster, hit harder, see better, hear more acutely, and jump higher than they could only seconds earlier.

The problem with the stress response is that the more it is activated, the harder it is to shut off. Instead of leveling off once the crisis has passed, your stress hormones, heart rate, and blood pressure remain elevated. Extended or repeated activation of the stress response takes a heavy toll on the body. The physical wear and tear it causes includes damage to the cardiovascular system and immune system suppression. Stress compromises your ability to fight off disease and infection, makes it difficult to conceive a baby, and stunts growth in children. It can even rewire the brain, leaving you more vulnerable to everyday pressures and mental health problems such as anxiety and depression. And, of course, the stress of living with a debilitating disease or disorder just adds to the problem.

Recent research suggests that anywhere from two-thirds to 90 percent of illness is stress-related. The following table lists some of the health problems that can be caused or exacerbated by long-term stress:

Health Problems Linked to Stress
- Heart attack
- Hypertension
- Stroke
- Cancer
- Diabetes
- Depression
- Obesity
- Eating disorders
- Substance abuse
- Ulcers
- Irritable bowel syndrome
- Memory loss
- Autoimmune diseases (e.g. lupus)
- Insomnia
- Thyroid problems
- Infertility

Coping with Stress

How to prevent, limit and manage its effects

Stress management and stress reduction techniques help you to cope with stress resulting from events like divorce, losing your job, children getting into trouble, caring for a sick relative, preparing for an exam, or just your daily commute.

What is stress management?

Stress is a normal physical reaction that occurs when you feel threatened or overwhelmed. The perception of a threat is as stressful as a real threat. You perceive a situation as threatening or feel overwhelmed because you are dealing with an unusually large number of everyday responsibilities. With increasing demands of home and work life, many people are under enormous stress. Stress in one setting can affect stress levels in the other.

The stress response narrows your ability to think clearly and function effectively. It can disable you physically and emotionally. The goal of stress management is to bring your nervous system back into balance, giving you a sense of calmness and control in your life.

Controlling your life means balancing various aspects of it — work, relationships and leisure — as well as the physical, intellectual and emotional parts. People who effectively manage stress consider life a challenge rather than a series of irritations, and they feel they have control over their lives, even in the face of setbacks.

There are no "one size fits all" solutions to managing stress. Every individual has a unique response to stress, so experiment with a variety of approaches to manage and reduce stress to learn what works best for you.

How can I change my lifestyle habits to manage stress better?

- Get enough sleep: Adequate sleep fuels your mind, as well as your body. Feeling tired will increase your stress because it may cause you to think irrationally.
- Connect with others: Develop a support system and share your feelings. Perhaps a friend, family member, teacher, clergy person or counselor can help you see your problem in a different light. Talking with someone else can help clear your mind of confusion so that you can focus on problem solving.
- Exercise regularly: Find at least 30 minutes, three times per week to do something physical. Nothing beats aerobic exercise to dissipate the excess energy. Physical activity plays a key role in reducing and preventing the effects of stress. During times of high stress, choose things you like to do. It also is

beneficial to have a variety of exercise outlets. Be physically fit in ways appropriate for your age, rather than being sedentary.

- Eat a balanced, nutritious diet: Be mindful of what you put in your body. Healthy eating fuels your mind, as well as your body. Take time to eat breakfast in the morning, it will help keep you going throughout the day. Eating several balanced, nutritious meals throughout the day will give you the energy to think rationally and clearly. Well-nourished bodies are better prepared to cope with stress..

- Reduce caffeine and sugar: Avoid consuming too much caffeine and sugar. In excessive amounts, the temporary "highs" they provide often end in fatigue or a "crash" later. You'll feel more relaxed, less jittery or nervous, and you'll sleep better. In addition, you'll have more energy, less heartburn and fewer muscle aches.

- Don't self-medicate with alcohol or drugs: While consuming alcohol or drugs may appear to alleviate stress, it is only temporary. When sober, the problems and stress will still be there. Don't mask the issue at hand; deal with it head on and with a clear mind.

- Do something for yourself everyday: Take time out from the hustle and bustle of life for leisure time. Too much work is actually inefficient and can lead to burnout. Recognize when you are most stressed and allow yourself some reasonable breaks. When things feel especially difficult, take a walk or change your scenery. Most importantly, have fun. Do things that make you happy.

How can I change my thinking and emotional responses to handle stress better?

- Have realistic expectations: Know your limits. Whether personally or professionally, be realistic about how much you can do. Set limits for yourself and learn to say "no" to more work and commitments.
- Reframe problems: See problems as opportunities. As a result of positive thinking, you will be able to handle whatever is causing your stress. Refute negative thoughts and try to see the glass as half full. It is easy to fall into the rut of seeing only the negative when you are stressed. Your thoughts can become like a pair of dark glasses, allowing little light or joy into your life.
- Maintain your sense of humor: This includes the ability to laugh at yourself. Watch a funny movie: the sillier the plot the better. The act of laughing helps your body fight stress in a number of ways.]
- Express your feelings instead of bottling them up: In order to live a less stressful life, learn to calm your emotions. A good cry during periods of stress, or sharing your concerns with someone you trust can be healthy ways to bring relief to your anxiety.
- Don't try to control events or other people: Many circumstances in life are beyond your control, particularly the behavior of others. Consider that we live in an imperfect world. Learn to accept what is, for now, until the time comes when perhaps you can change things.
- Ask yourself "Is this my problem?" If it isn't, leave it alone. If it is, can you resolve it now? Once the problem is settled, leave it alone. Don't agonize over the decision, and try to accept situations you cannot change.

How can I meet the challenges of stressful situations?

- Manage time: One of the greatest sources of stress is over-commitment or poor time management. Plan ahead. Make a reasonable schedule for yourself and include time for stress reduction as a regular part of your schedule. When you try to take care of everything at once it can seem overwhelming and as a result, you may not accomplish anything. Instead, make a list of what tasks you have to do, and then complete them one at a time, checking them off as they're completed.
- Give priority to the most important tasks and do those first: If a particularly unpleasant task faces you, tackle it early in the day and get it over with. You will experience less anxiety the rest of the day as a result. Most importantly, do not overwork yourself. Resist the temptation to schedule things back-to-back. All too often, we underestimate how long things will take.
- Schedule time for both work and recreation: Too much studying or working is actually inefficient and can lead to burnout.
- Delegate tasks and break up big projects: Being efficient and effective means you must delegate tasks and prioritize, schedule, budget and plan your precious time. Aim to work in short, intensive periods, which allow you to rest in between. Break big projects into smaller, more manageable tasks so you don't feel overwhelmed and nothing gets done as a result.

Stress relief technique
Description
Diaphragmatic breathing
(abdominal breathing)

Stress often causes our breathing to be shallow, which nearly always causes more stress because it puts less oxygen in the bloodstream and increases muscle tension. The next time you feel uptight, try taking a minute to slow down and breathe deeply. Breathe in through your nose and out through your mouth. Try to inhale enough so that your lower abdomen rises and falls. Count slowly as you exhale.

Progressive Muscle Relaxation (PMR)
Relaxation exercises help reduce anxiety and stress. First, you cause tension in certain muscle groups and then you totally relax them.

Meditation
Quiet the mind and engage in exercises that help you focus on your breathing, an object, or your body sensations. The goal is to relax the mind, body and spirit.

Practice Yoga for stress reduction
Yoga allows you to build up a natural response to stress and bring the relaxed state more into your daily life.

Practice Tai Chi for stress reduction
Tai Chi focuses on the breath and the mind's attention in the present moment.

Use massage for stress relief

A massage provides deep relaxation and improves physiological processes. As the muscles relax, so does your entire body, as well as your overstressed mind.

What are some more tips for coping with stress?

- Take a mental vacation: Take a moment to close your eyes and imagine a place where you feel relaxed and comfortable. Notice all the details of your chosen place, including pleasant sounds, smells and the temperature. Or change your mental "channel" by reading a good book or playing relaxing music to create a sense of peace and tranquility.
- Take a warm bath or shower: Wash the stress away and give yourself some time by yourself to reflect and quiet the mind. Soaking in the bathtub can make you feel like you are a world away from your reality.
- Use aromatherapy: Originating in ancient China, aromatherapy is based on the healing properties of plants; from which concentrated aromatic oils are extracted. The vapors of these "essential oils" are then inhaled and carried via the bloodstream, which controls the release of hormones and emotions.
- Care for a pet: Petting an animal can help reduce stress and lower blood pressure
- Keep a journal: One strategy that many people have found effective in coping with stress is keeping a journal, sometimes referred as a "stress diary." Writing thoughts down has a marvelous way of putting problems into perspective. Putting your worries into words may help you see that you don't really have that much to worry about, or it may help you get organized and manage your stress, rather than letting it manage you.

Keeping a journal should help you identify your concerns and establish a plan for moving forward. In your journal:

- List the situations that produce stress in your life (e.g., moving to a new location, work or school demands, balancing priorities, job promotion, etc.).
- Describe how you cope with each type of stressful experience.
- Evaluate your responses. Are they healthy or unhealthy, appropriate or unproductive?

When is professional help needed for stress management?

There's a fine line between feeling stressed out while still being able to function effectively, and the debilitating, even paralyzing phenomenon we think of as burnout or breakdown. The difference is between handling your stress on your own, and being unable to figure out what to do because the pressures of life have become so overwhelming. It's time to seek professional help if you:

- Feel that stress is affecting your health.
- Feel that it will never end.
- Feel so desperate that you think about quitting your job, running away, taking a drug overdose, or injuring yourself.
- Feel depressed, sad, tearful, or that life is not worth living.
- Lose your appetite and find it difficult to sleep.
- Are managing your stress level by eating, sleeping, drinking alcoholic beverages, smoking, or using recreational drugs.
- Have worries, feeling and thoughts that are difficult to talk about.
- Hear voices telling you what to do.

STRESS

"Then Jesus said to his disciples: 'Therefore I tell you, do not worry about your life, what you will eat; or about your body, what you will wear. Life is more than food, and the body more than clothes. Consider the ravens: They do not sow or reap, they have no storeroom or barn; yet God feeds them. And how much more valuable you are than birds! Who of you by worrying can add a single hour to his life? Since you cannot do this very little thing, why do you worry about the rest?'" (Luke 12:22-26, NIV; Matthew 6:25-34)

"I sought the LORD, and he heard me, and delivered me from all my fears"
(Psalm 34:4).

Connect all nine dots by using four lines and not picking up the pencil from the paper.

THE COLD WITHIN Six men trapped by happenstance In dark and bitter cold. Each one possessed a stick of wood, Or so the story's told. Their dying fire in need of logs The first man held his back, For on the faces around the fire He noticed one was black. The next man looking 'cross the way Saw one not of his church, And couldn't bring himself to give The fire his stick of birch. The third one sat in tattered clothes. He gave his coat a hitch. Why should his log be put to use To warm the idle rich? The rich man just sat back and thought Of the wealth he had in store. And how to keep what he had earned From the lazy, shiftless poor. The Black man's face bespoke revenge As the fire passed from sight. For all he saw in his stick of wood Was a chance to spite the white. The last man of this forlorn group Did naught except for gain. Giving only to those who gave Was how he played the game. The logs held tight in death's still hands Was proof of human sin. They didn't die from the cold without; They died from the cold within. -Author Unknown

I CRIED SO MANY TIMES, I WANT TO CRY... WHEN NO ONE'S AROUND, JUST TO HELP TIME FLY...

SO MANY NIGHTS, I WANT TO WEEP... ON LONG, LONG LONELY NIGHTS, WHEN I'M FEIGNING SLEEP...

SO MANY TIMES, TEARS HAVE ROLLED... WHEN THIS EMPTY HEART HURTS, FOR I HAVE NO ONE TO HOLD...

ON LONELY NIGHTS, WHEN I CAN'T REST... THE HUNGER IS SO, SO DEEP, FOR SOMEONE TO CARESS...

SOMEDAYS, MY EYES GET MISTY... BECAUSE IN MY CONFUSED MIND, I KNOW NO ONE MISSES ME... ONCE, I WANTED TO TELL THE WORLD GOODBYE... BUT I DID NOT, I JUST LAID THERE AND I CRIED, I CRIED...

Emotion 1. Defining Emotion Brainstorm and write definition of emotion Discuss how emotions are a form of communication 2. Perceptions of Anger Present the idea that anger is just an emotion that's been judged or perceived in a certain way; it is generally thought of as negative and something to be avoided at whatever cost. One way to understand anger differently is to challenge some of our perceptions. Function/Purpose of anger: message or indicator we send to ourselves that we're not happy. Need to know what to do with that message. Appropriate and inappropriate ways of dealing with anger. Point of workshop is to learn alternatives to communication and expression of anger.

Identifying Feelings

Intensity of Anger
Confused Furious Bewildered Enraged Trapped Outraged Troubled Aggravated Desperate Irate/ Spaced-out Seething Lost Elated Excited Overjoyed Thrilled Exuberant Fired-up Delighted High Medium Low Depressed Disappointed Alone Hurt Left-out Hopeless Sorrowful Crushed Heartbroken Down Upset Distressed Regret

CHECKLIST OF COGNITIVE DISTORTIONS

1. All-or-nothing thinking: You restrict possibilities and options to only two choices: yes or no (all or nothing). **2. Over generalization:** You view a single, negative event as a continuing and never-ending pattern of defeat. **3.** Negative **Mental** filter: You dwell mostly on the negatives and generally ignore the positives. **4. Discounting the positives:** You insist your achievements or positive efforts do not count. **5.**

Jumping to conclusions: Mind-reading: You assume that people are reacting negatively to you without any objective evidence. **Fortune-Telling: You** predict that things will turn out badly without any objective evidence. **6. Magnification or minimization:** You blow things way out of proportion or minimize their importance. **7. Emotional reasoning:** You base your reasoning from your feelings: "I feel like a loser, so I must be one." **8. "Mustabatory thinking" or "Shoulding All Over Yourself":** You criticize yourself or other people with "musts," "shoulds," "oughts," and "have tos." **9.** Labeling: Instead of saying "I made a mistake," you tell yourself "I'm an idiot" or "I'm a loser." **10.** Personalization: You blame yourself almost completely for something for which you were not entirely responsible.

Types of Problematic Thinking 1. Filtering: You take the negative details and magnify them while filtering out all positive aspects of a situation. **2. Polarized Thinking:** Things are black or white, good or bad. You have to be perfect or you're a failure. There is no middle ground, it's "all or nothing." **3.** Overgeneralization: Coming to a general conclusion based on a single incident or piece of evidence. If something bad happens once, you expect it to happen over and over again. **4. Mind Reading:** Without them saying so, you know what people are feeling and why they act the way they do. In particular, you are able to tell how people are feeling toward you. **5. Catastrophizing:** You expect disaster. You notice or hear about a problem and start "what ifs". 'What if tragedy strikes? What if it happens to you? **6. Personalization:** Thinking that everything people do or say is some kind of reaction to you. You also compare yourself to others, trying to determine who's smarter, better looking, etc. **7.** Control Fallacies: If you feel externally controlled, you see yourself as helpless, a victim of fate. The fallacy of internal control has you responsible for the pain and happiness of everyone around you. **8. Fallacy of Fairness:** You feel resentful because you think you know what's fair but other people won't agree with you. **9. Blaming:** You hold others responsible for your pain. Or, you take the other tack and blame yourself for every problem or reversal without regard to external causes. **10. Shoulds:** You have a list of ironclad "rules" about how you and other people should act. People who break the rules anger you and you feel guilty if you violate the rules. **11. Emotional Reasoning:** You believe that what you feel must be true automatically. If you feel stupid and boring, then you must be stupid and boring. **12.** Fallacy of Change: You expect that other people will change to suit you if you just pressure or cajole them enough. You need to change people because your hopes for happiness seem to depend entirely on them. **13. Global Labeling:** You generalize one or two qualities into a negative global judgment. **14. Being Right:** You are continually on trial to prove that your opinions and actions are correct. Being wrong is unthinkable and you will go to any length to demonstrate your rightness. **15. Heaven's Reward Fallacy:** You expect all your sacrifice and self-denial to pay off, as if there were someone keeping score. You feel bitter when the reward doesn't come.

• Having Other Family Members with Stress Problems (Stress is contagious.) • Pretending that nothing is wrong **Thoughts:** • This is horrible/unbearable. I'm not good enough. • I'm going to flunk out of school. I'm going to go crazy.

HOW VULNERABLE ARE YOU TO STRESS?

Mark from 1 (almost always) to 5 (never), according to how much of the time each statement applies to you. 1. I eat at least one hot, balanced meal a day. 2. I get 7 to 8 hours of sleep at least 4 nights a week. 3. I give and receive affection regularly. 4. I have at least one relative within 50 miles on whom I can rely. 5. I exercise to the point of perspiration at least twice a week. 6. I smoke less than half a pack of cigarettes a day. 7. I take fewer than five alcoholic drinks a week. 8. I am the appropriate weight for my height. 9. I have an income adequate to meet my basic expenses. 1O. I get strength from my religious beliefs. 11. I regularly attend club or social activities. 12. I have a network of friends and acquaintances. 13. I have one or more friends to confide in about personal matters. 14. I am in good health (including eyesight, hearing, teeth). 15. I am able to speak openly about my feelings when angry or worried.

16. I have regular conversations with the people I live with about domestic problems, e.g., chores, money, and daily living issues. 17. I do something for fun at least once a week. 18. I am able to organize my time effectively. 19. I drink fewer than three cups of coffee (or tea or cola) a day. 20. I take quiet time for myself during the day. SUBTOTAL - 20 = TOTAL To get your score, add up the figures. Then, subtract 20. Any number over 5 indicates a vulnerability to stress. You are seriously vulnerable if your score is between 25 and 55, and extremely vulnerable if your score is over 55.

MANAGING STRESS ACTION PLAN

Three of my major stresses which I can do something about: Three of my major stresses which I cannot do anything about or can do little about: My plan for the coming week to do something about one of the three stresses listed above which I have control over

Handling Your Stress 1. Pleasurable Activities A. By yourself (listen to music, take a walk, read a novel, TV) B. With others (do things with people you like) **2. Take Care of Your Body** A. Nutrition- avoid too much caffeine, nicotine, alcohol, drugs - eat healthy food: fruits, veggies B. Get adequate sleep C. Exercise!!! (Ideally 3+ times/week, 20-30 minutes) **3. Time Management** A. Check off tasks- make lists & have fun checking off as you get things done B. Prioritize C. Don't take too much on; know your limits **4. Maintain "Perspective"** A. "It's all how you look at it"; examine your thoughts for unhelpful! untrue thoughts-argue to yourself why they are incorrect/unhelpful; then substitute more correct/helpful ones **5. Communication Skills Getting Along with Others** A. Listen lots B Don't be passive, don't be aggressive, Be assertive **6. Laugh** watch funny movies, TV, look for the lighter side of life. **7. Relaxation** slow & deep breathing; imagine pleasant scenes; tense & relax muscles; music; reading; church/prayer/meditation... **8. Talk to Others about Being Stressed** (everyone is or has been!) A. friends, family B. Counselors **9. Read more on the subject:**

*The Holy Bible * The Relaxation & Stress Reduction Workbook * The Anxiety & Phobia Workbook * An End to Panic * Dying of Embarrassment * When Anger Hurts * Mind Over Mood

Regulating Emotions Present the idea that the goal of emotion regulation is not to get rid of emotions, but to increase our awareness of them. Present the idea that intense emotions have powerful immediate and aftereffects on our memory, thoughts, behaviors, and interpersonal relationships. Thus, it is important to learn how to manage and regulate our emotions. A. **First step in regulating emotions is**

identifying feelings Accurately label feelings; look at sheet for types of emotions Determine magnitude of feelings ; look at the level of intensity of emotion High-Low **B. Increase awareness of facial expressions & body changes C.** *Be* **"mindful"** Define: small shift in our awareness; becoming aware of our own experience, and state of mind. Mindfulness is being more aware of what we are experiencing in our mind and body from moment to moment. **D. Understanding Hidden Anger_** Present idea of proportionate and disproportionate responses to situations Discuss how residual left-over anger may be the result of previously unresolved situations, leading to "Hidden Anger."

Other causes for hidden anger may include: Unrealistic expectations Physical, emotional abuse Exposure to violence or abuse Greater sensitivity to stress 6. Self-Soothing Exercise__ Introduce deep-breathing as one technique for regulating emotions and managing hidden anger. **Mind-Body Connection** Present the idea that our bodies undergo a reflexive, physiological change, termed the fight or flight response, whenever we perceive a threat or believe danger is near. As a result, we are more likely to react impulsively to situations before we have time to think about the consequences. **Fight & Flight Response** Present information on the sympathetic nervous system, and how it is the body's way of preparing us for danger such as jaws clench, muscles tighten, heart rate up, blood leaves some of the main organs and goes to the extremities. Present the idea that our body , our physiology hasn't evolved as rapidly as society. We have the same physiology as we did thousands of years ago but our mind and society has developed tremendously (e.g. language). Ask participants to think of times when they have responded impulsively because of a perceived threat. **An Alternative to Fight/Flight is Mindfulness** Being mindful as opposed to going with impulses. We can use our mind to decide how we are going to respond to a perceived danger, rather than simply rely on our body. **Relationship between Stress and Anger** Present the idea that stress is cumulative, and doesn't automatically return to baseline. Ask participants to think of stressful events that may happen throughout the day, and graph it (wake-up late, miss bus, no coffee!) in order to demonstrate this point. Note that a person's baseline level of stress may be higher than usual due to factors such as illness or major life changes (e.g. marriage, graduation). Stress is cumulative the more stressed you are, the less it takes to get you to the overload point. You have a shorter fuse! It will take less to make you angry! The precipitating event may NOT even be something that would normally generate an anger response. Thus, it is important to notice if you're feeling especially stressed. Instead of just going about your day, it might be a better option to take some time to de-stress yourself.

Not anticipating/planning that you're going to get angry. Instead, anticipating that you *COULD* be quicker to anger, lose your cool, because you're stressed. By anticipating what *STRESSORS* might occur, you can assess your potential level of stress, instead of being surprised, frustrated and caught off guard. The goal is not to stress yourself out by your daily responsibilities, but to be aware of how those responsibilities can contribute to stress, and to plan ways to monitor and lower your stress (e.g. exercise, healthy diet, increase support). We can confuse our stress response with legitimate anger. Taking time to recognize when your life is particularly stressed allows you to assess what it is you're really feeling; this helps you to express yourself more authentically. If all stressful events evoke an "anger" response, then when you really are angry, you and others won't correctly recognize it, or won't respond appropriately. **1. Have a point(s):** What is the expected result of the confrontation? What is really making you angry? **2. Timing is Everything!** Plan a time to talk when you have plenty of time, privacy, and are feeling calm. **3. Stay Focused:** Keep your voice calm and steady; take long, steady breaths, take a "time out" if you feel yourself escalating; own-up to your feelings and beliefs. **4. Stay on Issue:** Only discuss the issue at hand. Don't get personal, insult or use foul language. Avoid making global accusations "you always/ never"; be specific in your concerns. **5. Compromise:** Agree to disagree; don't try to "win" or change someone's mind. Accept responsibility for your thoughts and feelings. Tolerate diversity and/or ambiguity. **1. Breathe deeply;** get your heart rate and breathing to a steady rate. Doing this in front of another angry person can also "model" this technique for them. **2. Remove yourself** from the situation if possible, and deal with it when you or they are feeling calmer or "centered." Let the other person know that you definitely want to talk, but at another time. **3. Reframe the situation;** consider another possibility for the conflict or outcome. Help others understand their anger by providing "plausible alternative reasons" for the situation. **4. Ignore personal attacks.** In the long run, it will gain you more respect. **5. Exercise Regularly.** Exercise allows your body to build up energy reserves and stimulates the release of endorphins; the body's natural calming hormones. Think of this as a preventative technique. **6. Violence is non-acceptable and not a solution,** unless you are being physically attacked. Violence can only be used against you and could have negative legal repercussions. If someone else attacks you, however, protect yourself Call 911 for reinforcements and to initiate legal protective action.

SELF-CONCEPT BUILDING A. List three ways to build personal accountability right where you are today. **EXAMPLE:** (Use this program; take control of my temper, etc.; quit blaming and be honest.) 1. 2. 3. B. List three things that could be used in your living space that would add a positive touch to the environment. EXAMPLE: (Pictures that remind you of what you want...the home, job, family, etc.; diary of positive or inspirational thoughts and ideas.) 1. 2. 3.

SELF

SELF TALK, SELF IMAGE

"…do you not know that your body is the temple of the Holy Spirit… and you are not your own? For you were bought at a price; therefore glorify God in your body and in your spirit, which are God's" (1 Corinthians 6:19-20, NKJV).

"…present your bodies a living sacrifice; holy, acceptable to God, which is your reasonable service" (Romans 12:1, NKJV).

Jesus Christ understands your pain. He grieves for you and longs to heal you.

"…we do not have a High Priest who cannot sympathize with our weaknesses… (Hebrews 4:15, NKJV).

"He heals the brokenhearted And binds up their wounds" (Psalm 147:3, NKJV).

He wants to turn your pain and suffering into joy and peace, and your fear and weakness into courage and strength in Him.

"Rejoice in the Lord always. Again I will say, rejoice! …Be anxious for nothing, but in everything by prayer and supplication, with thanksgiving, let your requests be made known to God; and the peace of God, which surpasses all understanding, will guard your hearts and minds through Christ Jesus…" (Philippians 4:4-9, NKJV).

"Be strong and of good courage, do not fear nor be afraid of them; for the LORD your God, He is the One who goes with you. He will not leave you nor forsake you" (Deuteronomy 31:6, NKJV).

"My soul, wait silently for God alone, For my expectation is from Him. He only is my rock and my salvation; He is my defense; I shall not be moved. In God is my salvation and my glory; The rock of my strength, And my refuge, is in God. Trust in Him at all times... Pour out your heart before Him..." (Psalm 62:5-8, NKJV).

Connect all nine dots by using four lines and not picking up the pencil from the paper.

How to Deal with Negative feelings: (1) Accept Them (2) Think and Act Opposite

He that is slow to anger is better than the mighty; and he that ruleth his spirit than he that taketh a city."--Proverbs 16:32

INEFFECTIVE STYLES OF DEALING WITH FEELINGS

Four Kinds: Control, Act-Out, Suppress, Feed CONTROL: You cannot control a feeling. Therefore, whenever you try to control a feeling all that you really accomplish is to give that feeling attention. Control includes attempts to: changes, become, develop, improve, and modify. The rule is: the feelings you resist persist. **ACT-OUT:** You often become frustrated with trying to control negative feelings because that only increases then. In order to get some relief from the energy of a negative feeling- -you choose to act-out that negative feeling. Even though you do get some immediate relief because the feeling is dissipated (released) from your acting it out--you have only reinforced that feeling. That is, the more you act-out a feeling the more you encourage it to return. This is why the ventilation, expression, or release of feelings is NOT a solution but only a short-term fix that leads to long-term problems. The rule is: what you act on you reinforce. **SUPPRESS:** You often avoid the experience of a feeling by suppressing it. Suppression and repression are just modern names for putting something into darkness. Repression means that you put it further into darkness than if you had only suppressed it. Darkness itself has also been renamed. Now we call the darkness within unconsciousness, preconsciousness, and semi consciousness. The results of suppressing or repressing a feeling are only that you are no longer aware of its impact on you. The suppressed feeling remains active and a driving force in your life. The rule is: what you suppress lives on in darkness. **FEED:** When you think thoughts and execute behaviors that are similar in nature to your feelings, you feed your feelings. Therefore, do NOT think anxious thoughts when you are anxious. Therefore, do NOT think angry thoughts when you are angry. Flee whining like the plague that it is. Flee worry like the pestilence that it is. The rule is: the feelings you feed grow. **AN EFFECTIVE WAY FOR DEALING WITH NEGATIVE FEELINGS**

Two Principles: Accept It—Think & Act Opposite ACCEPT IT: Since the only time to control a feeling is before it ever exists. The only seasonable course of action with an existing feeling is to accept it. The more unconditional or complete your acceptance is--the better. Let the negative feeling (anger, anxiety) dissipate (run out of energy) on its own. Let it go, be, flow. Detach from it. Disengage your identity from it. The rule is: the feelings that you refuse to make about your being will naturally pass. **THINK OPPOSITE:** Choose to will to think thoughts that are opposite in nature to your negative feelings of anger or anxiety. Always remember, you never have to think the way that you feel. By thinking the opposite of your negative feeling, you are creating sensations that will eventually lead to your feeling the opposite of your negative feeling. For example, when you are feeling angry or anxious your thinking calmly and rationally will eventually lead you to feeling calm and in control. The rule is: think against NOT for your negative feelings. **ACT OPPOSITE:** Choose to will to act the opposite from your negative feeling. Always remember, you never have to act the way you feel. By acting the opposite of your negative feeling, you are creating sensations that will eventually lead to your feeling the opposite of your negative feeling. For example, when feeling angry or anxious acting calmly will eventually lead you to feeling calm and in control. The rule is: act against your negative feelings.

Forgiveness Requires Forgiveness Unforgiveness is when you eat poison in the vain attempt to poison someone else. God will not be mocked. You must forgive to be forgiven. You bring into your life what you dwell on. Dwell on evil, whether of self or others, and you bring evil into your life. The hypocrite wants forgiveness but withholds forgiveness--so receives none. You have enough baggage to carry without carrying the sins of others. The evil of self or others that you resist letting go--persists in your mind. Is your mind a temple for evil or good? When you do not forgive it is because you want the other person to be damned. And you foolishly reason that your damning your internal images of them as some voodoo doll will keep them damned. In fact, it will. Only keep you damned for serving and hosting damning.

What is Worry Good For? "Peace I leave with you, my peace I give unto you: not as the world giveth, give I unto you. Let not your heart be troubled, neither let it be afraid."--John 14:27 Worry is a negative self-fulfilling prophecy. Worry is negative conditioning. Worry is negative expectation. Worry is negative intention. Worry is negative planning. Worry is negative prayer. Worry is negative programming. Worry is negative scripting. Worry is negative visualization. Worry is whining to yourself ahead of time.

Instead of worry do one of these three: 1) Pray 2) Problem-solve 3) Cope

4 Kinds There are four kinds of ego 1) **Spiritual** Identifying with the knowledge of comparisons of your spiritual knowledge, behaviors, and status with those of others: superior leading to spiritual pride and inferior leading to spiritual shame. 2) **Mental** Identifying with the knowledge of comparisons of your mental knowledge, behaviors, and status with those of others: superior leading to intellectual pride and inferior leading to intellectual shame. 3) **Social** Identifying with the knowledge of comparisons of your social knowledge, behaviors, and status with those of others: superior leading to social pride and inferior leading to social shame. 4) **Biological** Identifying with the knowledge of comparisons of your physical knowledge, behaviors, and status with those of others: superior leading to physical pride and inferior leading to physical shame. The worst is spiritual ego. Why? Because those who think they are good are not open to the correction they need to accept in order to repent and give up their ego. But any kind of well-established and fortified ego means that person has little chance of making it.

Moods, Happiness and Self Esteem A mood swing is a very important factor in decision-making and daily living. *Your state of mind is determined by your moods. In a positive state you are happy and enjoy the moment. Negative moods lead to misguided decisions, unhappiness and low self esteem.* **Negative thoughts only have power if you allow them to.** They are natural Don't make a mistake I've made, don't try to control your thinking, *control your reaction to thoughts,* Feeling low you are under pressure and time is running short, you panic. Everything looks serious. If you find yourself thinking like this, remember when everything seemed OK - Your life has not suddenly changed your attitude has. A mood can change your attitude and influence decision-making decide when you are feeling good. Emotions: Moods dictate how you see and react with the world. They color your perceptions and emotions warn you whether you are in a high mood and open to positive influence or whether you are in a low mood and thinking in your habitual way.

THE TRUE MEANING OF SELF-ESTEEM

Educators, parents, business and government leaders agree that we need to develop individuals with healthy or high self-esteem characterized by tolerance and respect for others, individuals who accept responsibility for their actions, have integrity, take pride in their accomplishments, who are self-motivated, willing to take risks, capable of handling criticism, loving and lovable, seek the challenge and stimulation of worthwhile and demanding goals, and take command and control of their lives. In other words, we need to help foster the development of people who have healthy or authentic sellesteem because they trust their own being to be life affirming, constructive, responsible and trustworthy. Unfortunately, efforts to convey the significance and critical nature of self-esteem have been hampered by misconceptions and confusion over what is meant by the term "self-esteem." Some have referred to self-esteem as merely "feeling good" or having positive feelings about oneself. Others have gone so far as to equate self- esteem with egotism, arrogance, conceit, narcissism, a sense of superiority, a trait leading to violence. Such characteristics cannot be attributed to authentic, healthy self-esteem, because they are actually defensive reactions to the lack of authentic self-esteem, which is sometimes referred to as "pseudo self-esteem." Individuals with defensive or low se1festeem typically focus on trying to prove themselves or impress others. They tend to use others for their own gain. Some act with arrogance and contempt towards others. They generally lack confidence in themselves, often have doubts about their worth and acceptability, and hence are reluctant to take risks or expose themselves to failure. They frequently blame others for their shortcomings rather than take responsibility for their actions. A close relationship has been documented between low self-esteem and such problems as violence, alcoholism, drug abuse, eating disorders, school dropouts, teenage pregnancy, suicide, and low academic achievement. However, it has been difficult to isolate it as a primary cause using traditional experimental research methods, for it is usually only one of several contributing factors. What needs to be stressed is that self-esteem is a critical component of any program aimed at sell-improvement or any rehabilitation program, for it is one of the few solutions that offers hope to correcting these problems. Many prisons, for example, have now - introduced self-esteem programs to reduce recidivism. One of the difficulties in trying to reach agreement on the nature of self-esteem is due to the fact that it has been approached from several different perspectives. Some have seen it as a psychodynamic, developmental process; others have approached it from the perspective of the cognitive-behaviorist in terms of various coping strategies; others have viewed it from the position of a social psychologist in terms of attitudes, while others have focused on the experiential dimensions of self-esteem as a humanistic psychologist. Since self-esteem has both psychological and sociological dimensions, this has made it difficult to come up with a comprehensive definition, N) and rarely have both dimensions been taken into consideration together in conducting research studies. There is, however, general agreement that the term self-esteem includes cognitive, affective, and behavioral elements. It is cognitive as one consciously thinks about oneself as one considers the discrepancy between ones ideal self; the person one wishes to be, and the perceived self or the realistic appraisal of how one sees oneself The affective element refers to the feelings or emotions that one has when considering that discrepancy. The behavioral aspects of self-esteem are manifested in such behaviors as assertiveness, resilience, being decisive and respectful of others. Thus, self-esteem is difficult to define because of these multiple dimensions. In addition, although self-esteem is generally stable, it can fluctuate from time to time, a phenomenon which is referred to as global versus situational self-esteem, and which can make measuring or researching self-esteem very difficult. It is important that the significance of self-esteem not be lost in the confusion over what it means. Self-esteem defined as "The disposition to experience oneself as being competent to cope with the basic challenges of life and of being worthy of happiness." The National Association for Self-Esteem modified this to define self esteem as "The experience of being capable of meeting life's challenges and being worthy of happiness." This concept of self-esteem is founded on the premise that it is strongly connected to a sense of competence and worthiness and the relationship between the two as one lives life. The worthiness component of self-esteem is often misunderstood as simply feeling good about oneself, when it actually is tied to whether or not a person lives up to certain fundamental human values, such as finding meanings that foster human growth and making commitments to them in a way that leads to a sense of integrity and satisfaction. A sense of competence is having the conviction that one is generally capable of producing desired results, having confidence in the efficacy of our mind and our ability to think, as well as to make appropriate choices and decisions. Worthiness might be considered the psychological aspect of self-esteem, while competence might be considered the behavioral or sociological aspect of self- esteem. Self-esteem stems from the experience of living consciously and might b. viewed as a person's overall judgment of himself or herself pertaining to self- competence and self-worth based on reality. The value of this definition is that it is useful in making the distinction between authentic or healthy self-esteem and pseudo or unhealthy self-esteem. A sense of personal worth without competence is just as limiting as competence without worthiness. A strong sense of worthiness prevents competence from becoming arrogance by keeping the individual focused on basic values, and competence prevents worthiness from becoming narcissism by requiring good feelings to be

Self-Esteem Descriptions These are general descriptions of how we feel when our self-esteem is high and how we feel when it is low, Those of us who fit either description on a regular basis know that our self-esteem is in tact or in need of work.

High Self-esteem Description: You "have a chronic case of feeling good." 1. You are generally not thinking about yourself and do not analyze yourself. 2. You feel good most of the time. When you feel bad, it doesn't last long. You are resilient in the face of diversity. 3. You smile a lot. You have positive belief systems about yourself, your family and society as a whole. 4. You have lots of energy. You are able to set and accomplish most of your goals. 5. You are friendly. You enjoy meeting and being with others. 6. You draw people to you. You make long-term friendships. 7. You look others in the eye. You are trustworthy and able to be intimate and affectionate. 8. You take risks. You are independent and autonomous. 9. You have positive effects. You have behavioral and academic success in school. 10. Things others cannot observe include: You talk to yourself positively, tell the truth, keep your word, are grateful to be alive, forgive yourself and others. You are empathetic, compassionate and you have a conscience. *The above actions, decisions about yourself and beliefs can be started and adopted at any time. They take lifelong practice and anyone can do them. A decision must be made, and then practice must begin. All of us make mistakes but being willing to forgive ourselves enables us to forgive others.*

Low Self-esteem Description:

Earned, not given. Thus, behaviors that might be described as egotistic, egocentric, conceited, boasting or bragging, bullying, taking advantage of, or harming others are defensive behaviors indicative of a lack of self .esteem. Such behaviors, therefore, should not be confused with authentic, healthy self esteem. Unfortunately, some of the confusion over the term self-esteem has stemmed from programs and strategies used that were not grounded in sound research. Such strategies include heaping children with undeserved praise not based on accomplishment. Most feel that it is critical that any efforts to build self-esteem, be grounded in reality. It cannot be attained by merely reciting boosters or affirmations, and one cannot give others authentic self-esteem. To do so is likely to result in an inflated sense of worth. Most feel that a sense of competence is strengthened through realistic and accurate self-appraisal, meaningful accomplishments, overcoming adversities, bouncing back from failures, and adopting such practices such as assuming self responsibility and maintaining integrity which engender ones sense of competence and self-worth. Is it possible to have too much self-esteem? We don't believe that it is possible to have too much true self-esteem, for having high self-esteem is equivalent to having good health. However, it is certainly possible for individuals to have an over-inflated sense of either worth or competence. Our objective is to develop individuals with high self-esteem that is well grounded in reality and balanced between an equal sense of worth and competence-- individuals who exhibit those qualities agreed upon by educators, parents, business and government leaders as essential to effective functioning in these changing times.

What is Self Esteem? Self esteem is the opinion you have of yourself. It is based on your attitude to the following: • Your value as a person • The job you do • Your achievements • How you think others see you • Your purpose in life • Your place in the world • Your potential for success • Your strengths and weaknesses • Your social status and how you relate to others • Your independence or ability to stand on your own feet I think this sums it up but you may be able to add a few other important factors I have not included here. **What is Low Self Esteem?** Low self esteem results from you having a poor self image caused by your attitude to one or more of the above Example you do not value the job you do highly or you feel you have no purpose in your life. Want to increase your confidence?

What is High Self Esteem? High self esteem is the opposite! It is a very important aspect of your life. If you have a high level you will be confident, happy and sure of yourself. You would be highly motivated and have the right attitude to succeed. Self esteem is therefore crucial to you and is a cornerstone of a positive attitude towards living.

You "have a chronic case of feeling bad." 1. You think about yourself a lot and analyze why you are the way you are. 2. You are stressful and fearful of adversity. You may be alienated from and in opposition with parents, caregivers and authority figures in general. 3. You do not smile easily. You may have a negative, hopeless view of yourself, your family and society. 4. You are tired a lot. You may be unwilling or unable to set and achieve your goals. 5. You stay to yourself. You prefer being alone to meeting new people or being with others. 6. You keep people away. You have trouble making and keeping friends. 7. You avoid looking into the eyes of others. You have difficulty with genuine trust, intimacy and affection. 8. You refuse to take risks. You are needy and may have a tendency to cling or to fake independence. 9. You create negative effects. And in extreme cases you can be antisocial and perhaps violent. 10. Things others cannot observe include: You talk to yourself negatively, you do not tell the truth or keep your word, and you do not forgive yourself or others. You may lack empathy, compassion and remorse. *Raising ones self-esteem takes changes in behavior. Behavior will change with practice and intention. Self-esteem is an achievement--a process that empowers, energizes and motivates. It is not something that we have, but the experience of things that we do. Self-esteem is the experience of being capable of meeting lfe 's challenges and being worthy of happiness.*

<u>Sell-esteem</u> Self-esteem is self as comparisons. Self-esteem is when you think you are good for doing good and bad for doing bad. Self-esteem is the duality of pride and shame. Self-esteem is when you are high (pride) when you compare yourself as better and low (shame) when you compare yourself as worse. Self-esteem is the modern name for ego. Ego is the phony self, a delusion in

Eastern psychology, and your spiritual enemy in Western traditions. Self-Esteem is a delusion since no one is or can be a comparison and self-esteem is self as comparisons. Self-esteem is the process of encasing and enclosing the identity in self-protective thoughts. Self-esteem is the experience of either ego pleasure or ego pain, Self-esteem is the duality of inferior and superior falsely applied to self. Self-esteem is the opposite principle from the principles of equality and universality. Self-esteem is the seeking of ego pleasure and the avoidance of ego pain. Self-esteem is when you irrationally identify with your behaviors and beliefs. Self-esteem is the fight-or-flight response to danger for ego and the seeking of safety for ego. Self-esteem is the delusional process of your seeking to become something, to die as thought. Self-esteem is the dualistic battle between wanting to always feel superior and still winding up feeling inferior. Self-esteem is you want to appear good and to avoid appearing bad. Self-esteem is when you delusional identify with your images of family, friends, groups, gods, and the like. Self-esteem is the process of inner conflict in which you try to do the humanely impossible: to transform the bad into the good. Self-esteem is when you are foolishly worried about being good or bad instead of doing good or bad. Self-esteem is the self-centered activity of creating your own Frankenstein monster from the dead bodies of other egos. Self-esteem is your collection of your superior and inferior comparisons of yourself, with your imagined selves for others, based on your imagined experiences for others. Self-esteem is self-idolatry. Self-esteem is a polite name for the mindless mental-chatter about what you are that devours your day. Self-esteem is the path of death as things. Self-esteem is the death of self as something and the disintegration of that thing as more things. Self-esteem is the name for the game of what things you should and should not be. Self-esteem is inner debate about what to put on your tombstone. Self-esteem is the royal road to death and destruction. Self-esteem is fear of opinion. Self-esteem is chimera chasing. Self-esteem is the practice of those who worship the god of opinion. Self-esteem is the way of attachment. Self-esteem is the battle to attach to pride and to detach from shame. Self-esteem is attaching to ego pleasure and detaching from ego pain. Self-esteem is the game of hiding shame with pride. High self-esteem is sadism and low self-esteem is masochism. -

Do You Really Want to Raise Your Self-Esteem? STEPS TO GET STARTED Make it your intent to: 1. Be on time for everything. You show respect for others and they will trust you. Those who respect others do not cheat, deceive or steal and are trusted. **2.** Be clean. Consistently groom your body, organize your space and donate to others. Nurture your body and your relationships and you will be confident. **3.** Say only supportive things to yourself Convert negative thoughts to think positively about yourself and others. You will be loyal. **4.** Keep your conscience clean. Talk to someone you trust. To confess is to heal. Have courage to do the right thing and you will build a good reputation. **5.** Take responsibility for your actions and choices—forgive yourself and others. Forgive and forget the incident and you will be tranquil. **6.** Put your desires in writing. You must know what you want to have it. Clarity makes one powerful. **7.** Be aware and appreciate the good in your life daily. This keeps you in the present and you will be gracious. **8.** Share your knowledge with those who wish to know. Contribute and participate and you will be joyful. **9.** Do what you love to do and do it where you want to be. You will be happy. **10.** Do what you say you will do, when you say you will do it, whether you feel like it or not. Keep your word and you will be reliable.

11 Tell your truth in the moment Don't wait for the "right" time You will be accountable for your choices. **12.** Be calm and alone for at least 24 minutes daily (one minute for every hour of the day). Pray, meditate or experience nature and you will be peaceful. *Self-esteem, as defined by the National Association for Self-esteem, is the experience of being capable of meeting life's challenges and being worthy of happiness.

"Failure lies not in the falling down but in the **staying** *down."* Author Unknown

The Challenge is Yours. What attitudes do I have that I might not see, but others do? How are they barriers between me and my vision? Am I looking at current reality? Have I made a personal commitment to stick with my vision, no matter what? List five escape routes and barriers causing me to live a lifestyle that is in conflict with my vision of freedom. 1. 2. 3. 4. 5. **TRIGGER TOOLS** In building resiliency and facing setbacks without giving up the vision, there are six trigger tools that are absolutely powerful. These six positive statements will crowd out negative self-talk and keep us focused on what we want.. .the vision. It is important to say these trigger tools over and over as you practice your vision in your simulator so that when negative setbacks occur, they will automatically enter your mind and keep you on track. **I AM I CAN I WANT TO I CHOOSE TO I LIKE IT I ACT NOW FLICK-BACK/ FLICK-UP** Another technique to build resiliency and help us keep the vision is the Flick-back/Flick-up technique. Again, as you experience your vision in the simulator in your mind, flick back to a time when you were very successful at something positive. Think about how that felt. Relive the experience as if it were happening again. Now flick up to your vision and bring with you all those successful feelings and apply them to how you feel when the vision is accomplished. This technique breathes life into the process of goal-setting and is crucial to success. Repeat this until it becomes automatic. Then when a setback occurs, instead of re-living the negative, you can flick back to that time and relive that instead.

How to Control Others "Be not angry that you cannot make others as you wish them to be, since you cannot make yourself as you wish to be. "--Thomas a Kempis To control others--control yourself To change the outer--change the inner. To get what you want--give what you want. When you change your responses, then others respond differently to your new behaviors. This is how you change or control others: indirectly through influence.

3 EFFECTIVE METHODS: You have three effective methods to change or control others:

1) **Example:** Model what you want. **2) Be available:** Practice active listening. 3) **Pray:** Pray for them to be under God.

3 INEFFECTIVE METHODS: You have many ineffective methods such that you can help them to be or do more of what you don't want. The big three are whining, blaming, and damning, or, if you prefer, nagging, scolding, and shaming.

WORST METHOD:

The worst method of all is perhaps the most common of all: negative motivation. Negative motivation is experienced as nagging, scolding, and shaming. For instance, if you want someone to be honest, then you accuse them of being dishonest all the time. Then when they are latter proved to be dishonest, you can say you knew it and you tried to prevent it. This is the favorite strategy of parents who ruin their children by calling them names and scripting them to be failures. "You will never amount to anything!" "You are a whore!" "You are a loser!" "You are stupid!" "You are evil!" "You are a bum!" Etc. Right intention coupled with wrong method = disaster

Is this behaving helping or hindering my feeling the way I want to feel? Is this behaving helping or hindering my acting the way I want to act?

3 Test for Practical Living_ SHORT VERSION OF 3 TEST Is this the way I want to think? Is this the way I want to feel? Is this the way I want to behave? Can I control others or life? NO! Then I had better control what I can most control--MY OWN THINKING! Now that I have controlled what I could--my own thinking--I now think, feel, and act more the way that I want to. Now others and life are responding to me differently!

LONG VERSIONS OF 3 TEST

THINKING Is this thinking helping or hindering my thinking the way I want to think? Is this thinking helping or hindering my feeling the way I want to feel? Is this thinking helping or hindering my acting the way I want to act?

FEELING Is this feeling helping or hindering my thinking the way I want to think? Is this feeling helping or hindering my feeling the way I want to feel? Is this feeling helping or hindering my acting the way I want to act?

ACTING Is this behaving helping or hindering my thinking the way I want to think?

Run a total of 25 miles by Sun. **1. Run** 3 miles each weekday 2. Run 5 miles daily on weekend **Three-Month Goal:** Save $1000 by _/_ **1.** Bank $200 each month **2.** Sell sofa for $400.00 **Six-Month Goal:** Learn WORD by _/_ 1. Hire computer trainer 2. Practice one hour each day **One-Year Goal:** Buy new car by _/_ 1. Sell car by July 1 2. Invest savings now **Five-Year Goal: Move to new area by** _/_ 1. Secure degree by 20_ 2. Get internship by 20_ "Sew a thought, reap an action. Sew an action, reap a habit. Sew a habit, reap a character, Sew a character, reap a destiny."

GOALS AFFECT OUR ATTITUDES AND OUR ATTITUDES AFFECT OUR FUTURE! What makes some people successful? Talents and abilities are important, but knowing what we want is equally important. When we know what we want, we can direct our energy and make choices toward the attainment of our specific goals. Attaining goals brings the setting of new goals, thus producing an on-going cycle of positive growth and achievement.

ACCENTUATE THE POSITIVE: Thinking positive and being positive can overcome the worst of situations. We can learn to live our lives in a productive positive manner by setting goals in writing. This solidifies them and gives us a concrete way of watching and experiencing them as they are met. Marking this progress and achievement becomes personally rewarding. It also builds strength, character and self-esteem. In setting goals we also list ways of achieving these goals. The plans for meeting goals are called objectives. In other words, objectives are measurable steps we take to reach our goals. **NAME POWER:** There is power in our names! Our names are our most valuable possession. We carry them around all of our lives, and they live on after we are gone. We make many choices throughout our lives and attach many things to our names. Our reputations are a culmination of our virtues, beliefs, actions, etc. and are all contained in our name. Others know us by our names. For example, someone may say, "Do you know Tony Brown? ' Another reply, "yes I do." Many things come to mind about Tony's personality as his name is brought to mind. Learn to hold your name high and attach only positive attributes to it! Set your goals to insure the reputation you desire. **PURPOSE:** An example of a life long goal = to keep my name powerful and positive. 1. Tell the truth to others and myself. 2. Keep my commitments to others and myself.

CREATING YOUR FUTURE GOAL SETTING: When setting goals, be specific. State the goal exactly as desired and visualize its completion. Write it as if already completed with dates and measurable results, such as: "I weigh (desired weight) by (date)". Then write your objectives to reach the goal, such as: A. Begin special diet. B. Jog two miles every other day. C. Join a support group. Pursuing goals is a method of consciously creating ones future. The way you are at 85 years old begins now with the setting of your goals. Review them every day of your life. Do it while you brush your teeth, when you go to bed and upon awakening in the morning. Visualize -- see yourself each day being, doing and having exactly what you want!

GOAL SETTING EXAMPLES TO FOLLOW: GOAL SETTING: When setting goals, be specific. State the goal exactly as desired and visualize its completion. Write it as if already completed with dates and measurable results, such as: "I weigh (desired weight) by (date)". Then write your objectives to reach the goal, such as: A. Begin special diet. B. Jog two miles every other day. C. Join a support group. Pursuing goals is a method of consciously creating ones future. The way you are at 85 years old begins now with the setting of your goals. Review them every day of your life. Do it while you brush your teeth, when you go to bed and upon awakening in the morning. Visualize -- see yourself each day being, doing and having exactly what you want! **GOAL SETTING EXAMPLES: Today's Goal: Clean my closet by 6 P.M.** 1. Sort all clothes by 3 P.M. 2. Re-organize closet by 6 P.M.

This Week's Goal:

Visualization

You may think that your intention is to help them experience the danger and pain of doing the wrong, but in the process you are identifying them with the wrong. Now, if they make the mistake of accepting your teaching, then they will be the wrong. And if they are the wrong, they will have to make it right. In other words, they will call evil good and accept the wrong as right, as self. **REAL CONTROL** 1) Control through acceptance. 2) Control through problem-solving. 3) Control through knowing when to use problem-solving or coping.

Emotional Maturity 6 Levels LEVELS 1-4 OF EMOTIONAL MATURITY

Level One Maturity -Basic Emotional Responsibility-

When a person reaches level one of emotional maturity, they realize that they can no longer view their emotional states as the responsibility of external forces such as people, places, things, forces, fate, and spirits. They learn to drop expressions from their speech that show disownership of feelings and a helpless or victim attitude towards their feelings. Expressions such as: "They made me feel. . . , ""It made me feel . . . ," "1 made them feel. . . ," and any others that denote external emotional responsibility are first changed into "I" statements as opposed to "You" or blaming statements. They are, for example, changed from, "You make me so mad when you do that," to "I feel mad when you do that because. People learn at this level to regularly use the following expressions: "When you did. I felt. . . , because. . . ." "When. . . happened, I felt. . . , because. . . ." As time and maturity advance, they begin to use even more accurate statements that inhibit the Blame Game such as: "I chose to feel. . . when I did. . . , because. . . ." "I choose to feel... whenever. . . happens, because. . . ." "I chose to feel. . . when he, she, it, did.. because. . . ." "I am in the habit of choosing to feel. . . whenever my/your. . . says anything to me, because. . .

Level Two Maturity -Emotional Honesty-

Emotional honesty concerns the willingness of the person to know and own their own feelings. This is a necessary step to self-understanding and acceptance. The issues of resistance to self-discovery are dealt with at this level. They are related solely to the person's conscious and unconscious fears of dealing directly with the critical voices they hear inside. In the past, they have typically lost all interactions with this internal adversary, so their fears are justified. Now, however, they know how to choose to feel so that they can keep from being destroyed, or they can choose not to interact with their accuser at all. The realization of the old maxim, "To thine own self be true," is the primary goal at this level. This means that we are always true to what we feel: we do not hide, stuff, suppress, or repress what we feel, but honestly experience it at this level of maturity. Here, you are at least honest with yourself about how you really feel. As a secondary goal on this level, people learn to locate others with whom they can safely share their real feelings, their real selves. Such work to never again accept self as behavior.

Level Three Maturity -Emotional Openness-

This level concerns the person's willingness and skills in sharing their feelings in an appropriate manner and at appropriate times. Persons at this level experience and learn the value of ventilating feelings, and also the dangers involved in hiding feelings from self and others. Self- disclosure is the important issue at this level of work. Yet, it will never be as important as the willingness of the person to be open to experiencing all of their feelings as they arise without the critical voices they hear inside trying to change, control, or condemn them. The dangers of suppressing feelings, and the values inherent in exploring and allowing all feelings internal expression are investigated further. At this level, one has the openness, the freedom to experience any emotion without the need, the compulsion to suppress or repress it.

Level Four Maturity -Emotional Assertiveness-

The person at this level of work enters a new era of positive self-expression. The primary goal here is to be able to ask for and to receive the nurturing that one needs and wants--first from self and then from others. As a secondary goal, persons should learn how to express any feeling appropriately in any situation, i.e., without aggressive overtones. This person makes time for their feelings--they prize and respect them. Such understand the connection between suppressed feelings, stress, and illness.

LEVELS 5-6 OF EMOTIONAL MATURITY

As I promised in *The Secret of Maturity,* this book contains levels five and six of the steps to complete emotional maturity. I cut them out of *The Secret of Maturity* and kept them for this book, because I didn't think they would be understood or appreciated without the explanations offered for self-concepts in this book.

Level Five Maturity -Emotional Understanding-

Persons on this level understand the actual cause and effect process of emotional responsibility and irresponsibility. Self-concepts are known as "the" problem. They realize that it is not possible to have a so- called good self-concept without a complimentary bad self-concept. Such experience firsthand, that because of the nature of knowledge and the formation of self-concepts, that all self-concepts contain their opposites. Knowing that though we may hide one half in darkness (unconsciousness) it is still active in us; they begin to regularly leap beyond the pitfalls of self-concepts, self-images, and self-constructs. This knowledge of the Unity of Opposites (of self-concepts, of knowledge) is applied to new situations daily. Other understandings at this level include the following: attempts to capture a moment of self can only kill the self as the self is a living process and not knowledge or memory; to reduce self to knowledge is literally to kill it; one either has their self and is alive and experiencing, or one has found their self as knowledge and lost it. Self-concepts are always externally referented by their very nature, and thus forever the perfect targets and hooks for the Blame Game. (For a description of the Blame Game see *The Secret of Maturity.*) Knowing that self-concepts are the only hooks that can be used in the Blame Game, people at this level remember to work on seeing their own self-concepts and finding release from their own. Self-knowledge is used to free the self from self-concepts on this level rather than to form them and imprison the self in them. The main work here is a total shift from identif'ing with any self-concepts to identifying only with the true self. II Corinthians 10:5 "Casting down imaginations, and every high thing that exalteth itself against the knowledge of God, . . ." Matthew 10:39 "He that findeth his life shall lose it: . .

Level Six Maturity -Emotional Detachment-

At this level the person lives without the burden and snare of self-concepts, self-images, self-constructs, and all group-concepts and thing-concepts. They are only aware of self as process, as a sensing being, as an experiencing being, as a living vessel, as unknowable and untrappable--because it is alive and not static or fixed. They have died to the life of self as self-concepts. True detachment from all self-concepts has occurred. Thus true detachment from others has also occurred, which means that absolute emotional responsibility has been achieved (actually discovered). Not having self-concepts to defend or promote, this person can remain unaffected by the Blame Game, and even experiences unconditional love for their enemies. I Thessalonians 4:4 "That every one of you should know how to posses his vessel in sanctification and honor;"

Maturity Maturity is when you face the fact that you are the enemy and NOT your parents, society, education, environment, food, conditioning, experiences, disadvantages, and-or hardships. Then and only then are you ready to begin to approach the problem rightly. And without the right approach, the best that you can do is to either substitute or mollify. Maturity is when your long-term intentions shape your short-term focus.

Self-Talk

The things you say to yourself, internal communication, or things you say to others that may or may not be positive. You may recall the good twin bad twin analogy discussed early in this program. At this time I would like to elaborate on this topic for a moment. Your brain doesn't know the truth from a lie. It will accept whatever you tell it over and over. If a child is told over and over again they are bad guess what they start to believe it and act accordingly. Your words, take on a life of their own so, be careful what you say. Your brain doesn't know what is true or false it simply processes the information it is given then stores the things which are repeated over and over again.

Food for Thought

You are a product of the people you associate with, the books you read and the TV shows and movies you watch. Be aware of what you let into your world because it will affect your success.

Affirming some things about you may not be healthy. For example you may say, "I am so forgetful," "I can't remember anything." Now, guess what you find yourself not being able to remember anything and you (your words) created that flaw. I can't say it enough, your words have power! Be careful what you say. In the same respect you have to be careful when it comes to people you associate with because you can find yourself falling prey to someone else's negative thoughts and feelings. You will want to protect your attitude and mental health at all times, at any cost. Your thoughts and words can make or break you.

WARNING!

You will not only want to watch what you say to and about yourself, you will want to be careful what you allow others to tell you about yourself. That doesn't mean you don't allow constructive criticism to be voiced, this is another form of personal growth. I am referring to mean, belittling, and hurtful things.

The Baseball Story

There were two men one was a professional baseball player and the other a prison inmate. The baseball player was being interviewed on the TV. The inmate was watching. The player was asked a question, "What is the one thing that you are the most proud of yourself for achieving?" The baseball player replied without hesitation, "I am most proud of the fact that I didn't disappoint my father." The interviewer asked him to elaborate. The player said, "From the time I was big enough to remember my dad always told me that I was going to be a GREAT baseball player one day and I would make it into the major league." The interviewer replied, "Your father must be proud!" "YES sir!" the player responded smiling from ear to ear. The inmate watching thought for a moment and jumped up from his set with excitement and said, "If that is the case then I am not so bad after all because I did not disappoint my father either. He always told me from the time I can remember that I was trouble and that one day I would end up in jail! Maybe I am not such a failure after all because I am exactly where my father always said I would be." Trust me your words have power!

5 Stages of
Self-Talk
Stage 1 Self-Talk

The stage of negative approval, the "I can't…..stage." This is the stage of self-destruction. This is the lowest and most harmful stage of self-talk. At this stage you say bad or negative things to yourself or someone else then you acknowledge it as fact. This stage of self-talk can be detected very easily. It is almost always distinguished by the follow words, "I can't…"

or "if only I could…" or "I wish I could, but I can't." This stage of self-talk always, always, always works against you. For example if you say, "I just don't feel up to doing the things I want to," "I don't know what's wrong with me I just can't seem to lose weight," "today is not my day," and "I just can't." In stage one these are normally the kinds of fears, doubts, and hesitations you feed your mind. It doesn't matter whether you say these things out loud or to yourself it is very damaging. Again, your brain doesn't know the truth from a lie, your subconscious mind will accept whatever you tell it and will go about its business to create or carry out the instructions received by you. Get out of this stage QUICKLY!

Stage II Self-Talk

The stage of observation and need to improve, the "I should…. and I need to… stage."

I refer to this stage as the self-deceiving stage. This stage is tricky. It might seem to work to your advantage, but it actually works against you. In this stage you know you are stating to yourself and others that you realize there is a need for change. But it creates no real solution for the problem. This stage of self-talk can be identified by the following statements "I need to…," or "I ought to…," or "I should…," (Mary Kay would always say "stop should'n on yourself"). When you say things like this to yourself or someone else you are sending mixed messages. Here is an example. "I really need to get more organized." You have just stated a fact, but your subconscious mind translates this as is "I am not organized." What you have said will not solve the problem, so our subconscious goes about creating what you told it, which was "I am not organized."

This stage works by making a statement that you need to change, you are not taking action on it, so the mind fills in the blanks with the negative programming from Stage 1 that it has been feed in the past. Here is another example "I would really like to earn more money....but I'm not!" "I would like to... but I can't." "I need to handle that...but I am not taking care of it." "I'd like things to work better....but they won't." These are the instructions you unconsciously send to your subconscious. Statements of this nature may seem harmless and powerless but they are very harmful and powerful. They affect your mental programming, thus your behavior, in a very non-productive manner. This programming controls your thoughts, actions, and attitude. You learned earlier that these things especially attitude can make or break a person. Stage II self-talk creates guilt, sadness, limitations in your abilities, and dissatisfaction. This is not a stage you want to be at for long.

Remember you subconscious will create whatever you tell it to that is why you must be very careful about what you say or feed you mind.

Stage III Self-Talk

The stage of decision making, you decide to change. I like to call this stage your stage of power. YES! This is the first stage that works in your favor. In this stage you recognize the need for change and you decide to take action toward making the change occur. You start to change yourself-talk, stating your decision to change in the "present-tense" as though the change has already taken place. This is known as the power of affirmations and visualization. Affirmations will be discussed in more detail later on in this program. Stage III is best distinguished by the words, "I never...," or "I no longer." In this stage you turn your negative thoughts into positive thoughts. For example instead of saying I would like to quite smoking... but I can't." You now say, "I never smoke!" Here are a few more empowering phrases. "I no longer have a problem with my co-workers." "I never eat more than I should." When your start working in Stage III, you will find yourself automatically beginning to reword old negative "can nots" in positive uplifting statements. When this happens, your subconscious wakes up the greatness that lies within you making the necessary change to fulfill your journey toward mental health, success, prosperity or whatever is your heart desires. Your subconscious is very, very, very, obedient it will do whatever you teach it to do.

You will find yourself using this stage on those occasions when you are working a practical change. This stage takes practice but when you make a conscious decision to use it, it will be very rewarding.

Stage III works because your mind doesn't know the truth from a lie. It accepts whatever programming you feed it, so learn to feed healthy nutritious food.

Stage IV Self-Talk

Stage IV the new and improved you, "I am....!" This is the first stage that unleashes your potential for success. I refer to this stage as operating in the law of attraction, the sky is the limit. You paint a visual picture with words that replace the old negative images and words. You describe how and what you want. This is one of the most powerful stages yet it is the least used. When you tap into the subconscious using this stage you will awaken the sleeping giant that lives within you. Embrace this stage with all your might; it is the beginning of your success journey.

Reprogramming in Stage IV self-talk sounds something like the following: " I am a winning!" "Only good things happen to me!" I believe in myself I know I can do anything I set my mind to do." "I am happy, healthy, and enthusiastic." Make the choice to use this stage often. You deserve the best. Decide to receive it today!

Stage V Self-Talk

The stage of self-unity, you are becoming one with yourself. This is the stage of completeness because you begin the journey to tap into your spiritual side to become one with your mind, spirit, and body. During this stage, you are pulling everything together: positive thinking, the power of visualization and affirmations. You are centering yourself in alignment with the universe (God) and spirituality.

I want you to think of yourself as a team made up of individual team members. For instance, team member one is positive thinking, team member two is positive self-talk, team member three is your deserve level, team member four is your attitude, team member six is your conscious, and team member seven is your subconscious. Now all of these team members are housed by your mind and work together to create your destiny or destruction. It all depends on how you coach your team to play the game. How things work within your mind is how it controls how you feel about yourself in your mind. When they are not in line, you operate more in the first two stages discussed earlier. Now at this stage you are learning how to get rid of the first two stages and start to affirm yourself in a positive uplifting way. Also you learn how to keep a healthy balance of mind, spirit, and body. I urge you to begin to use the self-talk of Stages III and IV. If it is right, Stage V will come in due time. Right now, learn the self-talk that will get you to work on time, help you maintain your family ties, give yourself the self-image you deserve and get the everyday things in life under control.

Creating new habits!

First of all I want to commend you for taking a courageous but necessary step to improve and enrich your life! WAY TO GO! I know by now you are probably thinking this is a lot of new stuff to learn. You are right but I believe in you, you can do it! Let me tell you a little secret. It takes 21 days to create a new habit. Twenty-one days of constant behavior modification to form new habits that will replace existing habits. So don't panic. It took time to form the habits you have right now. It will take time for you to learn new ones.

The skills and techniques you will learn in this program will not develop overnight. I know change is not easy, but "anything worth having is worth working for." After all your hard work you will emerge, like a lump of coal turning into a diamond.

Communication Skills
Basic Communication Skills Everyone Needs

Basic communication skills are required for nearly every job or relationship you pursue. What if you don't have time to take a writing course, or you are just too shy to speak up in meetings? That is OK. There are small steps that each of us can take with a little time, and little or no money. Let's take a look at the basic requirement most employers look for, and ways you can improve those skills.

Verbal Communication

The ability to speak clearly and concisely, and to convey information or articulate an opinion is essential for most jobs with internal or external customer contact. A good communicator is comfortable speaking to an individual or to groups.

If you wish to improve your verbal skills, you are not alone. Is it your speech, your language choice, or presentation style that you want to work on? To help you pinpoint it, ask a trusted colleague or manager to give you some feedback.

Speaking or diction courses at community colleges or adult schools will help you speak with confidence. You may also consider an acting or improvisation workshop, especially if fear of speaking is an issue for you. Many people join Toastmasters to take their speaking and presentation skills to a new level.

Speaking skill is just as important when you're talking one on one as it is when you addressing one hundred. There are dozens of seminars on the subject of effective communication, relationship building, sales calling or serving customers. In one day you can begin to change the way you communicate with individuals.

Written Communication

The ability to convey your message in writing using proper grammar is a basic requisite for nearly every job. Once you have control of grammar, you can work to enhance your style.

Most community colleges offer evening courses on the subject of grammar or writing. Many offer both creative writing as well as business writing.

Go to your local teachers supply store for grammar or writing self-study workbooks. They may be geared toward high school students; however, they are inexpensive, self-paced, and portable. I have used these workbooks in training courses, and they are highly effective for building basic skills.

Find someone who is an excellent writer, and ask them to be your writing coach. Meet to review one of your writing samples and re-write it together. With a good coach, you will make quick progress.

Go online and search for online writing courses. Check your favorite search engine using keywords such as 'distance learning', 'writing', 'online courses'.

Listening

The ability to listen carefully and understand the speaker's message is key to building relationships and succeeding at work.

Focusing your full attention on the speaker is a good start. However, if you want to develop your listening skills, we suggest you check out audiotapes or videotapes from your local library. There are quite a variety of tapes in this category. You may also check out 'books on tapes' establishments.

Sharing Your Opinion or Analysis

At some point you'll be asked to share your opinion and explain how you came to that opinion. You may even need to defend your opinion in a cool, concise way.

Listen to others, and pay attention to how they express themselves. Be aware of your company culture, and stay within that framework.

A fun way to improve this skill is to listen to talk radio shows that feature controversial issues. If you scan your AM dial during drive time, you're sure to come across one. You'll hear many articulate people sharing and defending their view. You may even feel compelled to call in and try your skills with the host.

Find a mentor. Role play with your mentor and ask for candid feedback.

Most times when you are asked your opinion at work, it is regarding a subject you are close to. Relax and share your experience. Be confident in yourself because you are the expert on what you do.

All forms of communication are a reflection of your professionalism, your intellect, your preparedness, and your character. You'll never be sorry you took the time to develop your communication skills.

Basic Communication Skills

As you speak with a person, not only are you sending them verbal messages through what you say, you are also sending them non-verbal messages through your posture, facial expression, and tone of voice. It is important that your verbal and nonverbal messages are complementary and supportive of each other. There is a simple acronym for these non-verbal messages, ROLES

R - Remain RELAXED with your peer
0 - Adopt an OPEN position
L –LEAN toward your peer at times
E - Maintain good EYE contact
S - Face your peer SQUARELY

Aspects of Listening/Attending

1. Physical attending or the physical aspects of listening means doing some things and not doing others to show that you are involved with, and available to, the other.

a) Facing the other squarely not turning to the side.

b) Maintaining good eye contact -- look directly at the other. This does not mean staring down the other, rather, communicating through eye use in a warm way that you are genuinely interested and involved.

c) Be aware of the distance from the other. Some experimentation may be necessary determine the optimum distance.

d) Try to have an "open" posture. Crossed arms and legs might make the other feel you are not really approachable or maybe that you do not want to get involved. Be aware of what your gestures are saying to the other.

e) Be aware of the environment. It may be too light or too dark, conducive to getting the other to relax or not. A radio or stereo may be distracting Attempts should be made to minimize outside disturbances or interruptions. Having a desk or other objects between you and the other may give the impression of not being fully available or approachable.

f) Leaning or moving toward the other, at least at appropriate times may indicate to the other your presence, warmth, interest, and willingness to be there.

g) Try to be relatively relaxed and comfortable yourself while still being alert and attempt to make the other comfortable also.

2. Monitoring and perceiving what the other is verbally saying.

a) As the conversation progresses, try to remember in detail what the other has said. Track exact content in your mind.
b) Look for common themes. Often the other will make the same points in different ways.
c) Pay attention to unusual words or words that are repeated as they may be significant. Some research has shown that what is said immediately after the word can be very important. Contradictions, confusion, and anxiety may be found in the phrase that follows.
3. Non-Verbal perception:
a) The way manner, or style in which the voice and words are used can be crucial. You should be alert to the tone of voice, loudness, pitch, inflection, spacing of words stumbling over words, emphasized words, and pauses.
b) Facial and body movements can be extremely communicative particularly of the emotions and feelings of the other.
c) Non-verbal cues obviously can confirm, emphasize, or modify what is said in the verbal message or sometimes they can contradict the verbal content and convey the true message. A verbal "yes" may really be "no," as reflected by facial expression, tone of voice, etc.
d) The Importance of non-verbal behavior is illustrated by Mehaorian's findings in 1971. He found that in an inconsistent message delivered, the receiver tended to define its meaning according to the following percentages: verbal 7%, way and manner of verbal delivery 38%, and facial 55%. In other words, if facial behavior contradicts verbal behavior, the facial expression will dominate the impact of the total message, with the actual verbal content having the least effect of the three categories studied.

4. Stance for effective helping.

a) You should be alert for why you are there. What is the reason for listening? Sometimes the real reason is not apparent until the conversation has been going for several minutes.

b) You need to concentrate and focus as much as possible on all verbal and non-verbal cues the other is giving. This involves resisting distractions both external and in your own head, and focusing on the other -- a-difficult task!

c) Try to be non-judgmental about what the other is saying, at least initially. It is difficult to really listen to the other while putting our own values on everything being said.

d) Be aware of the uses of pauses and silence. Practice waiting, as sometimes your comments may cut off something important that the other may be getting ready to say. Conscious practice of waiting will develop a sense of when pauses are most productive.

e) You should encourage the other to talk about feelings and behavior with minimal words and comments yourself. Sometimes a gesture, nod, or one word comment are most effective. This can also help the other feel that you are appropriate, not mechanical or phony.

f) It is essential to communicate verbally and non-verbally to the other that you are interested and listening. The other may need clear signals or feedback from you

g) Not to be neglected in the listening/helping relationship is the need to monitor and listen to yourself as well. Self-listening enables you to deal in the immediate moment to follow how you are affecting the other and perhaps why.

Forgiveness

Guilt, anger, shame, and hate are feelings you feel when you have done something that you feel is unjust to someone else or yourself. These feelings of pain are the silent punishment that you place on yourself. Sometimes we find it hard to forgive our self because we know all the wrong, unjust acts you have committed. When you chose not to forgive yourself it hinders your deserve level. Which makes it hard for you to accomplish your true hearts desires; forgiveness will increase your deserve level. Cut yourself some slack, after all you are human. Plus you can only do better, once you have learned to better yourself. Think of your moments of unjust behavior as stepping-stones for learning. Now you are becoming the person you have envisioned. When you refuse to forgive yourself you choose to continue to hold on to the painful feelings discussed earlier. Just because you forgive yourself doesn't mean you are letting yourself off the hook. It means you come to a point in your life where you feel the pain of blaming and hating yourself is enough. The pain you feel must end! Let go of your past, this must be done in order to move forward towards your journey of long-term success and mental health.

Forgiving Yourself and Others

There is a great deal of confusion about what it means to forgive and about how to do it. Hopefully these ideas, which over the years I have discovered work best for my clients and for myself, will also be valuable for you.

To forgive another person does not mean you will forget what happened or that the person is not responsible for what he did or that you need to bring him back into your life. To forgive another doesn't even need to mean the other person knows you've forgiven him or her. To forgive another simply means you no longer allow another person's actions or words to cause you resentment, anger and pain. To forgive means you acknowledge that while you would have preferred the other person act or speak differently, you accept that person just as he is.

To not forgive another means you continue to hold onto your resentment, anger and pain over another's actions by essentially demanding the other person be someone other than who that person knew (or knows) how to be.

To forgive yourself does not mean that you should forget what you did or said that might have injured another or caused yourself distress. To forgive yourself doesn't mean you aren't responsible for what you did or said. To forgive yourself simply means you realize that you might have done something differently if you had known how. Forgiving yourself means you recognize that you didn't know how to do something differently and realize you have learned by your mistake. As someone once said, experience is what we get right after we need it. To forgive yourself means you are finally willing to accept yourself just as you were at the time you made the mistake you've been holding over your head.

To not forgive yourself means you continue to hold onto guilt and pain and demand the impossible -- that you be someone other than yourself, other than who you were when you hadn't yet learned the lesson you gained from your mistake.

If you would like to practice a forgiveness exercise (and it can take a bit of practice), consider whether the following might work for you in considering what someone has done to you.

Imagine the person who has offended you in some way is standing in front of you as he was when he said or did something hurtful and say something like this:

"When you said or did _____ , I was hurt and angry. I would have preferred you _____ . But you did not. When I think about what you said or did, I have let myself feel anger, resentment, pain, bitterness. I have held onto my demand that you should have said or done something different. I no longer choose to hold onto the tension and hurt that accompanies my memory of what you said or did."

"Therefore, I cancel the demands, expectations and conditions I placed on you that you should have ____ . You are totally responsible for your own actions and deeds."

"I now send my love or (if that word is too strong) acceptance to you as a human being, just as you were and are now."

Then imagine that your love or acceptance is going out to the other person. Take your time to experience how your body feels when you release the conditions you placed on this person to be someone he did not know how to be or, for whatever reason, was unable to be.

This kind of forgiveness exercise recognizes the amount of power you have over other people's actions -- that's right, YOU DON'T HAVE ANY. While you can have strong preferences that someone behave in a certain way, you cannot control another person no matter how much you might demand they act as you would want them to -- and no matter how reasonable those expectations may seem to you and to anyone who agrees with your position. They are responsible for their actions and you are only responsible for yours. Holding tightly to the expectation that others behave as you would have them behave is contrary to the way things work and thus unnecessarily stressful.

When you are through with the exercise, allow relief to seep into every pore of your body as you release your demand that others be someone they are not.

To use this same kind of forgiveness exercise for yourself can also be very healing.

You can begin to forgive yourself by realizing that when you made the mistake(s) for which you now criticize yourself you did not wake up in the morning and deliberately set out to mess up your life or to harm someone else. If you had known how to make better choices, you would have. At the time you did the best you could. Therefore, you can forgive yourself by using words similar to those above and applying them to yourself. Imagine you are saying them to the person you were in the past, even if the past was a short time ago.

As you say those words, allow yourself to be both the giver and receiver of forgiveness, letting that love flow through every part of your body. Feel the release of tension that comes from forgiveness.

Self - Image
Matters
Dress for your seat at the top!

Developing a strong positive self-image is crucial to your success. Your image is your personal billboard to the world! What does yours say about you? Dress for the position you want to have not the position you have or are trying to obtain. You only have 30 seconds to make a good first impression. The opinion formed about you in these 30 seconds rarely ever change. Always make your 30 seconds count! People see what you wear on the outside as a reflection of how you feel about yourself on the inside and the world around you. Is yourself-image sending the wrong message? Your appearance can also be interpreted as how effectively and affectively you will handle business for a prospective employer.

Dress for your raise to the top!

- Proper Attire
- Skirt length- for a short skirt the length should be at the knee or no shorter than 2" above the knee when seated. Long skirts should fall below or at the ankle when seated.
- Dress pants or suited pants- you will want to make sure your pants are not to tight or to short. One rule of thumb when purchasing pants is buy them one size larger than your real size. This way they will be more comfortable and slimming to your figure. NO BLUE JEANS!
- Suit jacket- make sure the sleeves are not to short or to long on a long sleeve jacket. Preferably lying at the end of your wrist. If it is a short sleeve jacket it should end in the middle of your bicep or right below it.
- Blouse- NO TANK TOPS! Short or long sleeve blouses only same rule applies for your blouse as your jacket in reference to sleeve length. Don't wear clothing that is to small or to revealing.
- Shoes- your shoes should always be clean and shined. No tennis shoes, and no open toed or opened heeled shoes. No flats, you will want to wear a 2" to 2 ½" heel. If you can't wear a heel that high try wearing a 1" heel. They look better than flats. If you have marks on your shoes simply take a little finger nail

polish remover on a cotton ball and rub it on your shoes, it will usually remove the marks.
- Panty hose- Yes! Hose should be worn even in the summer. Make sure they fit. The way you can tell if they fit is around the ankles; if you see little creases or excess material they are too big. If you pull them all the way up and they don't fit in the seam area they are too little. One more thing about panty hose. Your hose should never be darker than the color of your shoes. Example: Black panty hose should be worn only with black shoes. Your panty hose should always be lighter than your shoes.
- Fabric Material
- Correct clothing- wear the right fabric for the right season. No wool in the summer and no linen in the winter.
- Shoes- No white shoes after Labor Day. White shoes are in season only between Memorial Day and Labor Day.
- Colors- you will not want to wear real bold, loud, or weird colors. You will not want to distract from your personality by the color of your outfit. Wear colors that make you feel confident.
- Jewelry- you will want to stay from wearing big, bold, noisy jewelry. Keep things small, simple, and conservative.
- Hygiene
- Odors/Fragrance- Bathing and deodorant prevents unwanted body odor, no heavy perfumes, wear light fresh clean perfumes. Perfume should be applied to pressure points. One squirt behind each ear and one on each wrist.

- Oral Hygiene- always brush your teeth and maintain proper oral health care.
- Skin Care- healthy skin exhibits overall wellbeing. After all your face is one of the first things people see, take care of it! Healthy skin is a sign of pride and confidence. After all if you are not willing to take care of your skin on a regular basics how can you take care of business issues daily?
- Nail Care- you will want to keep you nails clean and well manicured. Stay away from wild designs and loud crazy colors. If you wear color on your nails make sure there are no chips in your polish at anytime if you do chip a nail fix it immediately. If you have false nails keep them up or take them off.
- Hair- your hair should always be neat and clean. No unnatural colors such as blue, purple, or green. However, this doesn't mean that you can't have bottled blonde. No screaming roots! When it is time for a touch up take care of it ASAP!
- Color Cosmetics- your make-up should appear natural. You will want your lips, eyes, cheeks, and nail color to be from the same color family as your clothing. For example: warm with warm and cool with cool. I can assist you more later if you would like to have a personal makeover and learn more.

Key factors to make the law of attraction work for you:
- Know what it is that you want.
- Ask for what it is that you want.
- Believe that you will receive it.
- Be aware and open to receiving what it is that you want.

- Live each day on purpose-plan, focus your thoughts on what it is that you desire.
- Visualize yourself obtaining your desires.
- Be thankful for things that you currently have and for the things to come in the future.
- What you receive will be a product of your thoughts, that you fuel with emotions and repetition.

Let's revisit our garden for a moment.

Seed- is the way you were when you entered the Blossom program.

Roots- your positive support system is the positive family members and friends you have in you life.

Soil- is your foundation, your utilization of the tools and techniques learned in this program.

Water- positive affirmations

Sunshine- daily modification of your behaviors and thoughts

Stem- your growth during this program

Keynote: The stem of a plant or flower is where food travels and it is part of its support system to hold it up.

Leaves- life lessons; in the day-to-day activities of life is were you stretch and grow.

Keynote: The leaves are where life is sustained it gives off oxygen and makes chlorophyll which is necessary for plant growth.

Petals-show a true form of balance and growth.

Positive Thinking!
Dealing with you!
Why is positive thinking important?

You are what you think. Your deepest most repeated thoughts become your reality. I have learned that our thoughts and some feelings often operate on a subconscious level. Bringing awareness to your thoughts and feelings can lead to a more productive, happy, joy-filled existence. When you develop the habit of positive thinking you can control the outcomes of your life. It has been said that you can be a dream maker or the wrecking crew in the development of your life. It all lies within our own thoughts.

The biggest difference between people is their attitudes. Your attitude, your way of thinking is a habit. The great thing about habits is old ones can be replaced with new ones. Our attitudes are maintained by the internal self-talk and conversation that we have with ourselves. When you change yourself-talk and internal communication, you begin the process of changing you attitude. You will take baby steps to change your internal communication. Now let's review the "Checkup from the Neck Up" steps:

1st Decide
You must make up your mind that this is something you want to accomplish. Commit to working on your development everyday.

2nd Focus
Stay tune into what it is that you want and desire. Keep your eyes on the goal even when things seem unclear. Make visual aids to help keep your mind on what you want to achieve, look at it often.

3rd Action

Feed your brain daily with positive, motivating uplifting things. Associate with positive people. I know you are thinking, "But what about my friend Jane she is so negative. Does it mean that I have to stop being friends with her?" No, but you may want to monitor the amount of time spent with her. WARNING you become like the people you associate with. In this situation you will either rub off on them or visa verse so be very careful.

Keys to developing a positive mental attitude
- Look for positive things in yourself as well as others
- Associate with positive people
- Look for the good in every situation (As Mary Kay always said " keep the lesson, throw away the experience)

Remember: your thoughts and feelings become your reality!!!!

Your Brain

People have referred to the brain as many things, for example the brain is like a computer it takes in whatever you put into it. The brain is a mini tape recorder. It records and plays back things at certain times. All of these analogies are true but I would like to take it one step further. I want you to think of your brain as a garden.

To truly develop a positive way of thinking you have to attend to your mental health everyday. It cannot be something you do only on occasion.

Your brain is the dirt/soil; your thoughts are the plants that need to be tended. A garden is something that needs physical and mental energy. It needs to be worked on almost everyday. When you decide to develop a positive mental attitude you will need to actively work on it everyday.

Your thoughts need the same maintenance. I refer to this as weeding the garden. Daily you will need to tend to your garden, remember the Checkup from the Neck Up. You want to read or listen to something positive everyday. Replace any negative thoughts with positive uplifting ones.

Daily you will want to focus on things for which you are grateful. I refer to this as watering your garden. Focus on things that make you happy. Focus on positive outcomes instead of focusing on what you don't want to happen.
You reap only what you plant nothing more, nothing less. Be careful what you plant.

Reciting positive affirmations daily is very important. I refer to this as the beginning, deciding what you are going to grow. Are you going to grow the reality of hope, success, prosperity, and happiness or are you going to grow self-destructing thoughts of hopelessness and failure? You can't plant potatoes in a garden and expect tomatoes to grow. It is the same way with the brain. You can't plant thoughts of defeat, negativity, failure, and misery and expect to receive peace of mind, success, happiness and a positive self-worth. You must make a decision everyday to wake up and grow your reality of success and happiness.

Strengthening Your Inner-self!

You have the power and strength that you have not even thought of using. Once you step out of your comfort zone you will be amazed at the power you pose inside. I know you are asking, "Okay Ursulette, if I have the ability to change and all of this inner power how can I develop it and start using it to improve my life?" I am so glad you asked. The following are key points to tap into your unused power within:

- The ability to dream and visualize. Can you dream like you did when you were a little girl? Do you even remember what your little girl dreams were? I challenge you to free your mind and dream again. Here is an exercise that may help, close your eyes imagine you are a little girl. Describe what you look like out loud. You have to be very specific. What does your outfit look like, how are you wearing your hair? Describe things that might have been around you. Let your words give so much detail that you see everything in your mind's eye. Another way to build this skill is to get your favored magazine, and look at a picture that you find appealing. Look at it for about 10 to 20 seconds. Once you are done close your eyes and describe the picture to yourself out loud and while you are talking try to see the picture in your mind.

- You never quit when you were a baby learning how to walk. Did you quit because you kept falling? No, you kept trying until you learned how to stand on your own two feet, put one foot in front of the other and walk. Guess what? You can make a decision and stick to it until you achieve it.

A big shot is just a little shot that just keep right on shooting.
- Mary Kay

- Make a firm decision and stick to it
- Learn to motivate yourself to accomplish what you want. Don't wait on someone else to tell you that you can do something. Push yourself, because in reality you are all you have. Choose to depend on yourself. Anything the mind can believe it can achieve.

- Believe in you. Have faith in yourself and in your abilities. When you have confidence in yourself it builds courage, which makes it easier for you to step out of your comfort zone. Reach for the stars, you are liable to catch one.

- Discipline yourself. You must learn to discipline yourself. If not, someone else will discipline you for the rest of your life. You must not give into your temptations. Commit and stand firm. In the end you will be reward greatly. Instant gratification lives up to its name. It is pleasure that you receive for an instant then it vanishes. To achieve long- term gratification you must understand short-term sacrifice for long-term gain. I will give up a little today to gain a lot tomorrow.

Time Management And Goal Setting
Time Management

Good time management skills and tools when used properly can greatly reduce your stress level. When your have a plan of action in place you are less likely to forget what it is you have to do and therefore you will reduce the stress in your life.

Goal Setting
What do you have planned for your life?
Goal Areas

Spiritual

Family

Career

Physical

Social

Educational

Financial

Your goals in all of these areas must align with each other for you to have long-term success.

Create a Balance
Think of yourself in two layers the first being the core, the second the outer layer. You want to create a balance within the core part of your being. Once this has been established

the other areas will develop on their own. When I say create a balance I do not mean that you have to give everything the same amount of time. You must put your priorities in order; spiritual (faith) first, family second, career third. When things are in that order of balance you will have true harmony.

Do your goals in these areas coincide with your heart's desire? If not, are you willing to change some things in your life to achieve your true heart's desire? Keep in mind when your purpose is clear the price you pay is never too high, when your purpose is unclear the price you pay is always too high.
Balance does not mean equal
Your Vision

Where do you see yourself in the next five years?

_____

_____

_____

_____

_____

_____

What do you want out of life?

_____

_____

_____

_____

_____

_____

What will your success look like? You must be able to see it in order to achieve it.

_____

_____

_____

_____

_____

_____

Personal Vision and Mission

Vision: your vision is what you see for yourself and family (where you see yourself going, the big picture), it is something that excites, motivates, and provokes people to enroll their efforts, time, and skills into developing your mission and success.

Create a Vision Statement

When creating your vision statement you may want to consider the following.

1. What are your priorities and beliefs?
2. What do you value?
3. How will your pass these principles on to others?
4. If you were guaranteed not to fail what would your success look like? Be very specific; what kind of house will you live in, what type of car will you drive, where will you go on vacation, what kind of clothes will you wear? You need to go into detail about each of the things so that you can start to see your success.
5. What are your hopes, goals, and dreams?
6. In your wildest dream what would you have, be or do if you were successful?

Mission: mission statement is your plan of action, your belief system and the steps you plan to take to achieve the vision.

Create a Mission Statement

When creating your mission statement you may want to consider the following.

1. What do you want to contribute to your community, society, and or individuals?
2. How or what do you want to be remembered by when your are no longer around?
3. How will you be an asset to the world?
4. How do you plan to influence and affect people, and your community?
5. How do you plan on impacting your circle of peers for the better good of man kind?

Your "Dash"

We have very little control over some things in our lives. We had no control over the day we were born, who our parents are, what color or heritage background we have, or the day we die. When you look at someone's tombstone all you see is the date they were born a dash and the date they died. All of their experiences, choices, ups and downs are in that "dash."

When you think about what you want to do with your "dash" what do you see? You can choose to take control of your life and live it in the most fulfilling way possible.

Attitude

Attitude is the most important element in the development of a positive and healthy state of mind. Attitude is your perception (how you see things) of a given situation or event. Attitude is more important than facts. It does not matter how many facts you have about a situation, if your perception of that experience does not change the facts are irrelevant.

We are very emotional beings. Often negative attitudes or negative self-talk is a habit that is developed as a defense mechanism. More often than not we talk ourselves out of certain situations because they make us feel uncomfortable or nervous. When we begin to experience these feelings the negative self-talk begins. Instead of working through this internal communication and replacing it with positive self-talk we often talk ourselves out of taking action.

Research shows people allow past experiences to keep them from living up to their full potential. They feel that they do not have control of the outcome; no matter what history will repeat itself. The human mind is powerful and we can change the outcome of any situation but we have to want to. We have the mental power to do and
To become victorious over negative thinking, you must gain and keep control over the things you say to yourself.

Win the war against stinkin' thinkin'.
change anything we decide to change. That is the key, we first must decide! Then we have to change our attitudes and our internal self-talk. Internal self-talk is the communication (talk) that goes on in your mind. This communication is

the most powerful form of communication we have with ourselves. It can lead to victory or disaster. With this in mind you must learn to control and manage what you think and say to yourself. Some refer to this as the "chatterbox in your head". The chatter can cause your attitude to shift from positive to negative and from negative to positive.

I want you to pretend that you have twins, one good twin this one always has positive uplifting thoughts and things to say. The bad twin (evil twin) on the other hand is constantly saying mean doubtful non-positive things, which causes you to think unhealthy thoughts. When this happens I want you to lift up your hand and flick the evil twin off your shoulder and say, "Cancel, cancel." I want you to visualize him/her rolling down your back hitting the floor. This image will cancel your negative image or thought. You will be able to continue on with your day and journey towards success and mental health.

Check up from the neck up!
Developing a healthy mental attitude is a day-to-day, minute-by-minute battle. I feel that this battle is a lot like that battle that alcoholics go through. Everyday an alcoholic has to choose not to drink and some days when stress is at an all time high they (the alcoholic) may find that it is a minute-by-minute or even second-by-second battle. It is the same with the process of developing a healthy mental attitude. You must daily do a check up from the neck up take a mental inventory of your thoughts, emotions, and words. You can do this check up by completing the following steps everyday. You may find yourself doing it five, six, seven times a day until a positive mental attitude becomes a habit for you. Even then you will want to do the following steps at least three times a day this will help make this habit very strong.

Here are the steps

1st Decide

Everyday you must decide that having a healthy mental attitude, success, and prosperity is what you want out of life. You must commit to working on your development <u>DAILY!</u>

2nd Focus

Stay in tune with what you want out of life. Keeping your eyes on the desired outcome and not on what is going on at that practical moment. There will be times that things seem dark and dreary, you will not want to give your time and energy to those things. "Keep your eye on the prize" as they say. If you do this you will be rewarded greatly. Visual aids will help with this part of your daily check up. We will discuss the use of visual aids and their importance later on in this program.

"You can do everything right with the wrong attitude and not succeed but you can do everything wrong with the right attitude and still succeed!" - Mary Kay

A positive attitude is one of the most valuable assets you can possess.

3rd Action

Feed your brain daily with positive, motivating, and uplifting things. Associate with positive people. This completes your daily checkup!

Hang around
Winners!

Now just like with anything else that you learn, you must practice to become good at it. Guess what? You will need to practice these skills as well to develop a healthy mental attitude and a more balanced positive way of life.

I know what you are thinking all my friends are negative or my friends are going to think that I am a nerd for buying into all this positive thinking, self-improving, changing your life crap. It is okay, you can invite them to learn with you by you sharing what you have learned. If they are not willing to learn you will not want to cut them out of your life altogether but you will want to monitor and limit your time with them.

The attitude of your friends are like the buttons on an elevator. They will either take you up or the will take you down!

Remember: you become like the five people you associate with the most. A word of wisdom if you don't want to trade places with them then take their input about what you are doing to improve yourself and your way of life with a grain of salt. In other words, don't give a lot of validity (weight) to their opinion. You and only you can change your destiny.

ATTITUDE
By Charles Swindoll

The longer I live, the more I realize the impact of attitude on my life. Attitude, to me, is more important than facts. It is more important than the past, than education, than money, than circumstances, than failures, than successes, than what other people think or say or do. It is more important than appearance, giftedness or skill. It will make or break a company ... a church ... a home. The remarkable thing is we have a choice every day regarding the attitude we will embrace for that day. We cannot change our past ... we cannot change the fact that people will act in a certain way. We cannot change the inevitable. The only thing we can do is play on the string we have, and that is our attitude ... I am convinced that life is ten percent what happens to me and ninety percent how I react to it. And so it is with you ... we are in charge of our attitudes."

Connect all nine dots by using four lines and not picking up the pencil from the paper.

Affirmations

Group affirmation
I am a person of integrity, strong character, and a positive healthy mental attitude. I have an abundance of income; I always have more money coming in than going out. Good health and prosperity is my destiny.

What are affirmations?
Statements that describe what you want using positive words that change your thought process. Affirmations make all things possible. They are the commands that program the thought and words you feed your mind. If you think negative thoughts you will receive negative results. If you think positive thoughts, success, health and wealth will follow. It doesn't happen in a couple of day. Affirmations must be repeated often at least three to five times each day. When saying your affirmations you must have belief, emotion, and enthusiasm. Your emotion, belief, and enthusiasm trigger the subconscious mind to act and carry out what you are telling it.
List three areas of improvement. (Activity)
1.
2.
3.
In closing, thinking is a combination of words, sentences, mental images, and sensations. Thoughts are visitors who visit the central station of the brain. They come, visit and then disappear making room for other thoughts. It is very

important to be careful of what goes into the subconscious mind. Words and thoughts that are repeated frequently get stronger by repetition. Repetition allows thoughts to sink into the subconscious mind, which affects your behavior, actions, and reactions. Your thoughts and words you express mold your life. When you allow outside circumstances and situations to influence your thought process you have no freedom. To regain your freedom you must learn to prevent negative circumstances from influencing or controlling your thinking. Positive affirmations allow you to regain control of your situation, instead of your situation controlling you.

Affirmations Using Bible Verses

These are the affirmations for a better you.

I can see the Kingdom of God because I am born again. John 3:3

I don't worry about everyday life. God knows my needs and meets them because I make His Kingdom my primary concern. Matthew 6:25-33

Jesus shows himself to me because I love him. John 14:21

Because Jesus died for my sins, I am no longer separated from God. I live in close union with him. Romans 5:10

The fruit I produce brings great joy to God, my Father in Heaven. John 15:8

God's power works best in my weakness. 2 Corinthians 12:9

Through the energy of Christ working powerfully in me, I teach others His truths. Colossians 1:29

I have been saved, not by works, but grace, so that I might do good works. Ephesians 2:9-10

My faith makes me whole in spirit, soul and body. Mark 5:34

When I call out to God He answers me. He tells me things I wouldn't know otherwise. Jeremiah 33:3

Because I place my hope in the Lord my strength is renewed. Isaiah 40:31

As I follow Jesus.....as I walk with him, I have peace. Luke 24:36

Because I obey Jesus I remain in his love. John 15:10

The cross of Christ is my power. 1 Corinthians 1:17

My God meets all my needs. Philippians 4:19

God is my refuge and strength .... always ready to help me in times of trouble. Psalm 46:1

God gives me strength when I am weary and increases my power when I am weak. Isaiah 40:29

Because I place my hope in God, I can soar like an eagle, run and not grow weary, walk and not be faint. Isaiah 40:31

I set my heart and mind on things above, not earthly things. This gives me peace. Colossians 3:1-2

I guard my heart because it determines the course of my life. Proverbs 4:23

I trust God at all times because he is my refuge. Psalm 62:8

As I lose my life for Jesus' sake, I find it. Matthew 10:39

God keeps me in perfect peace because I trust in Him and fix my thoughts on Him. Isaiah 26:3

God is able to do immeasurably more in my life than I could ever imagine. Ephesians 3:20

I experience true life when I deny myself, turn from my selfish ways and follow Jesus. Matthew 16:24-25

I have the anointing of Jesus, through the Holy Spirit. He teaches me truth and empowers me to live a full life. 1 John 2:27

I could not experience an abundant life except for Jesus and the cross. Matthew 16:24

I love God's principles and meditate on them all day long. Psalm 119:97
I live by faith, not by sight. 2 Corinthians 12:7
I follow Jesus, no matter where he leads me. Matthew 6:20
The same love that God has for Jesus is in me. John 17:26
I am being made holy by God's truths. John 17:17
It is by the grace of God and his love that I am saved by my faith. Ephesians 2:5
I can approach God directly with freedom and confidence through faith in Jesus. Ephesians 3:12
I worship the Lord my God and serve only him. Luke 4:8

Truth Affirmations
- I am joy, peace, love, hope, serenity, humility, kindness, benevolence, empathy, generosity, truth, compassion and faith.
- I get stronger each passing day
- Doors to truth and love are opening for me.
- My mind is filled with thoughts that bring love, light and truth to my life.
- Truthful expression is a healing and strengthening force.
- I am energized by truth and love.
- By living in the present I acknowledge truth in my life. That strengthens me.
- I take positive actions which support my own blessed truth..
- I am filled with the Love of the Universal Divine Truth.
- I communicate clearly and consciously from my deepest truth.
- I tell the truth with integrity and compassion.

- My deepest truth sustains me continuously.
- Everything happens for my highest good.
- I am responsible for myself
- Flexible curiosity allows me to discover endless truth.
- My life is lived, exuberantly, consistently, and creatively, in That Love.
- "For the law was given by Moses but grace and truth came by Jesus Christ." - John 1:20
- I embrace truth and the best always works out for me because of this.
- I am a student of my own soul and search deeply for my real truths.
- Being myself involves no risks. It is my ultimate truth, and I live it fearlessly.

Heart Affirmations

- I am in a loving and passionate relationship
- I touch others with a soft, kindhearted smile.
- God lives inside my heart!
- I listen with my own compassionate, loving heart as others share their own stories.
- I open my heart to the wisdom, love and compassion of the Christ.
- I take positive risks and I am willing to share from the treasuries of my own blessed heart and mind.
- I open my own blessed heart to mercifully receiving and accepting all others just as they are.
- Lord Jesus I humbly ask you to come into my heart and dwell within me.
- I remain focused on my Heart's desires and take inspired actions to fulfill them.
- I fully trust the clarity of my own blessed heart.

- I follow the bliss of my own heart's true, blessed desire.
- I follow my own heart's true, blessed eternal living wisdom.
- Blessed harmony is the true heart of community.
- Intuitive answers come to me spontaneously, simultaneous with my own heart's true, pure desire.
- Knowing what I am not, and remembering who I am, brings peace and joy to my heart and mind.
- My music moves people's hearts
- My mind and my heart are in perfect agreement.
- I open my own blessed heart to all that is possible.
- Lighthearted laughter is liberating.
- True wisdom is in the true deep heart.

Gratitude Affirmations

- I gratefully accept all the health, wealth and happiness that the universe pours into me every day.
- I gratefully accept all the wealth and happiness that the Universe pours into me every day
- I approve and love of myself, I am healthy, beautiful, loving, giving, I give thanks for all that I have and all that I shall be. I am open to all possibilities. I have abundance in all areas of my life; I begin again and again, to reinvent myself daily.
- I am thankful for all the love in my life
- I am happy and grateful for everything I have and receive daily
- I breathe in gratitude and breathe out love
- I am grateful for my health
- my life is abundant and amazing right now!
- I am thankful for God's endless treasures.

- I see all of the beauty and grace which is around me with loving gratitude.
- I am thankful for all the good in my life
- I am thankful for my blessings. I focus on the good things in my life thereby giving them power to grow and multiply.
- I am receiving abundance every day
- I am grateful for all that I experience in this lifetime
- I appreciate all, I show my gratitude, I give thanks.
- I am very profoundly thankful for my own unique and wonderful life.
- I start each day with a gratitude attitude
- I give thanks and choose to be happy
- I am releasing the past and appreciating the present.
- THANK YOU UNIVERSE!

Bottom of Form

Virtue Affirmations

- I will exercise order in my life. I will let all things have their places. I will let each part of business and lives have its time.
- I shall tolerate no un-cleanliness in body, clothes, habitation or thought.
- I will practice sincerity in all I do. I will not be hurtful or deceitful. I will think innocently and justly. I will speak accordingly.
- I will exercise moderation in all I do. I will avoid extremes.
- I will exercise the virtue of silence. I will speak not but what my benefit others or myself. I will avoid trifling conversations.
- I will exercise chastity and be known as a person of virtuous character. I will never use venery to dullness,

weakness, or the injury of my own or another's peace or reputation.
- I will exercise the virtue of frugality. I will make no expense but to do good to others or myself. I will waste nothing.
- I will practice humility through the imitation Jesus and Socrates.
- I will seek justice for all. I will wrong none by doing injuries or omitting the benefits that are my duty.
- First Cardinal Virtue: Reverence for all life
- I live by the Second Cardinal Virtue: Natural Sincerity
- I live by the First Cardinal Virtue: Reverence for all life
- I live by the Fourth Cardinal Virtue: Supportiveness

Recap

Recapitulate
What are two stages of self-talk that benefit you the most?

_____

_____

What happens to the brain when you learn something new?

_____

_____

What is Attitude?

_____

_____

What are the three steps to perform the check up from the neck up?

_____

_____

_____

5. Why do you feel having a positive attitude is important?

_____

_____

_____

_____

_____

6. What are positive affirmations?

_____

_____

_____

_____

7. How many times should affirmations be repeated?

_____

List three signs of self-sabotaging behavior:

_____

_____

_____

List two things that you can do when you feel yourself about to carry out a self-sabotaging behavior:

_____

_____

List the five key points to strengthen your inner-self:

_____

_____

_____

_____

_____

11. How long does it take to create a new habit? _____

What is your dominant learning style?_____

How will using what you have learned during this program help you on your success journey?

_____

_____

_____

_____

_____

What one thing have you learned thus far that has benefited you the most?

_____

_____

_____

_____

_____

List the components of complete positive mental health.

_____and_____
+
_____and_____
+
_____and_____
+
_____and_____

Define the law of attraction.

_____

_____

_____

_____

6. What are the two stages of self-talk that benefit you the most?

_____

_____

7. What happens to the brain when you learn something new?

_____

_____

What is Attitude?

_____

_____

What are the three steps to perform the check up from the neck up?

_____

_____

_____

10. Why do you feel having a positive attitude is important?

_____

_____

_____

_____

_____

11. What are positive affirmations?

_____

_____

_____

_____

_____

12. How many times should affirmations be repeated?

_____

List three signs of self-sabotaging behavior:

_____

_____

_____

List two things that you can do when you feel yourself about the carry out a self-sabotaging behavior:

_____

_____

List the five key points to strengthen your inner-self:

_____

_____

_____

_____

_____

16. How long does it take to create a new habit? _____

17. What are the two stages of self-talk that benefit you the most?

_____

_____

What happens to the brain when you learn something new?

_____

_____

What is Attitude?

_____

_____

What are the three steps to perform the check up from the neck up?

_____

_____

_____

21. Why do you feel having a positive attitude is important?

_____

_____

_____

_____

22. What are positive affirmations?

_____

_____

_____

_____

23. How many times should affirmations be repeated?

_____

List three signs of self-sabotaging behavior:

_____

_____

_____

List two things that you can do when you feel yourself about the carry out a self-sabotaging behavior:

_____

_____

List the five key points to strengthen your inner-self:

_____

_____

_____

_____

_____

27. How long does it take to create a new habit? _____

What is anger?

_____

_____

List three physical signs of anger.

_____

_____

_____

List three emotional signs of anger.

_____

_____

_____

What are some common anger management techniques?

_____

_____

_____

Identify the three categories of stressors.

_____

_____

_____

What is stress?

_____

_____

_____

List three ways stress can affect your mind.

_____

_____

_____

List 3 emotional symptoms of how stress can make you feel.

_____

_____

_____

What are some of the physical effects that stress can have on your body?

_____

_____

_____

_____

_____

What are some ways stress can affect your behavior?

_____

_____

_____

_____

_____

What are the three types of stress?

_____

_____

_____

What are the long term effects of stress?

_____

_____

_____

_____

_____

What are some techniques for stress relief?

_____

_____

_____

_____

_____

List three tips of coping with stress.

_____

_____

_____

What is fear?

_____

_____

_____

What is your dominant learning style?_____

How will using what you have learned during this program help you on your success journey?

_____

_____

_____

_____

_____

What one thing have you learned thus far that has benefited you the most?

_____

_____

_____

_____

_____

List the components of complete positive mental health.

_____ and _____
+
_____ and _____
+
_____ and _____
+
_____ and _____

Define the law of attraction.

_____

_____

_____

_____

21. What are to two stages of self-talk that benefit you the most?

_____

_____

22. What happens to the brain when you learn something new?

_____

_____

What is Attitude?

_____

_____

What are the three steps to perform the check up from the neck up?

_____

_____

_____

25. Why do you feel having a positive attitude is important?

_____

_____

_____

_____

_____

26. What are positive affirmations?

_____

_____

_____

_____

_____

27. How many times should affirmations be repeated?

_____

List three signs of self-sabotaging behavior:

_____

_____

_____

List two things that you can do when you feel yourself about the carry out a self-sabotaging behavior:

_____

_____

List the five key points to strengthen your inner-self:

_____

_____

_____

_____

_____

31. How long does it take to create a new habit? _____

32. What are to two stages of self-talk that benefit you the most?

_____

_____

What happens to the brain when you learn something new?

_____

_____

List two things that you can do when you feel yourself about the carry out a self-sabotaging behavior:

_____

_____

List the five key points to strengthen your inner-self:

_____

_____

_____

How long does it take to create a new habit? _____

The CENTER of ALL

Q: What is the shortest chapter in the Bible? A: Psalms 117   Q: What is the longest chapter in the Bible? A: Psalms 119   Q: Which chapter is in the center of the Bible? A: Psalms 118   Fact:There are 594 chapters before Psalms 118

Fact: There are 594 chapters after Psalms 118   Add these numbers up and you get 1188.   Q: What is the center verse in the Bible? A: Psalms 118:8   <u>Psalms 118:8</u> (NKJV)   "It is better to trust in the LORD than to put confidence in man."

~ AMEN ~

"As for me and my house, we will serve the Lord"

The Lord's Prayer

Our Father,
who art in heaven,
hallowed is thy name.
Thy Kingdom come,
thy will be done,
on earth as it is in heaven
Give us this day our daily bread.
And forgive us our trespasses,
as we forgive those who trespass against us.
And lead us not into temptation,
but deliver us from evil.
For thine is the kingdom,
The power and the glory,
Forever and ever.
Amen.

The Serenity Prayer

God grant me the serenity
to accept the things I cannot change;
courage to change the things I can;
and wisdom to know the difference.
Living one day at a time;
Enjoying one moment at a time;
Accepting hardships as the pathway to peace;
Taking, as He did, this sinful world
as it is, not as I would have it;
Trusting that He will make all things right
if I surrender to His Will;
That I may be reasonably happy in this life
and supremely happy with Him
Forever in the next.
Amen.

Psalm 23 of David.

The Lord is my shepherd;
I shall not want.
He maketh me to lie down in green pastures:
He leadeth me beside the still waters.
He restoreth my soul:
He leadeth me in the paths of righteousness
for his name's sake.
Yea, though I walk through the valley of the shadow of
Death,
I will fear no evil:
for thou art with me;
thy rod and thy staff they comfort me.
Thou preparest a table before me
in the presence of mine enemies:
thou anointest my head with oil;
my cup runneth over.
Surely goodness and mercy shall follow me
all the days of my life:
and I will dwell in the house of the Lord for ever.

APPENDIX

The Race

Author Unknown

Quit! Give up! You're beaten! They shout out and plead.

There's just too much against you, now, this time you can't succeed.

And as I start to hang my head in front of failures face

My downward fall is broken by the memory of a race.

And hope refills my weakened will as I recall that scene

For just the thought of that short race rejuvenates my being.

A children's race, young men, young boys. Oh, I remember it well.

Excitement, sure, but, also fear, it wasn't hard to tell.

They all lined up so full of hope, each through to win that race

Or tie for first or if not that at least take a second place.

And fathers watched from off the side, each cheering for his son.

And each boy hoped to show his Dad that he would be the one.

The whistle blew and off they went, young hearts and hopes afire

To win, to be the hero there was each young boy's desire.

And one boy in particular, his Dad was in the crowd,

Was running near the lead and thought, "Oh, my Dad will be so proud."

And as he speeded down the field, across a shallow dip

The little boy who thought to win, lost his step and slipped.
Trying hard to catch himself, his hands flew out to brace
And mid the laughter of the crowd, he fell flat on his face.
So down he fell and with him hope, he couldn't win it now,
Embarrassed, sad, he only wished to disappear, somehow.
But, as he fell his Dad stood up and showed his anxious face
That to the boy so clearly said, "get up and win that race."
He quickly rose, no damage done, behind a bit, that's all
And ran with all his mind and might to make up for his fall.
So anxious to restore himself, to catch up and to win
His mind went faster than his legs, he slipped and fell, again.
He wished that he had quit before with only one disgrace,
"I'm hopeless as a runner, now, I shouldn't try to race."
But, in the laughing crowd he searched and found his father's face
That steady look that said again, "Get up and win that race."
So he jumped up to try again, ten yards behind the last.
"If I'm going to gain those yards," he thought, "I've got to run real fast." Exceeding everything he had, he regained eight or ten
But trying so hard to catch the lead, he slipped and fell, again.
Defeat! He lay there silently, a tear dropped from his eye.
"There's no sense running, anymore, three strikes, I'm out --- why try?"
The will to rise had disappeared. All hope had fled away.
So far behind, so error prone, closer all the way.
"I've lost so what's the use?" he thought. "I'll live with my disgrace."

But, then he thought about his Dad, who soon he'd have to face.

"Get up!" An echo sounded low, "Get up and take your place."

"You were not meant for failure, here. Get up and win that race."

With borrowed will, "Get up!" it said, "You haven't lost at all."

"For winning is not more that this, to rise each time you fall."

And so he rose to win, one more. And with a new commit
He resolved that win or lose, at least he wouldn't quit.
So far behind the others, now, the most he'd ever been,
Still he gave it all he had and ran as though to win.
Three times he'd fallen, stumbling; three times he's rose, again.
Too far behind to hope to win, he still ran to the end.
They cheered the winning runner as he crossed first place
Head high and proud and happy - no falling, no disgrace.
But when the fallen youngster crossed the line in last place

The crowd gave him the greater cheer for finishing the race.

And even though he came in last with head bowed low, not proud,

You would have thought he'd won the race to listen to that crowd.

And to his Dad he sadly said, "I didn't do so well."

"To me you won" his father said, "you rose each time you fell."

And when things seem dark and hard and difficult to face
The memory of that little boy helps me in my race.
For all of life is like that race with ups and downs and all

And all you have to do to win is rise each time you fall.
"Quit! Give up! Defeat!" They still shout in my face.
    But, another voice within me says, "get up and win that race!"

Shoelaces Parable

    First, let us assume that you have a poor way of tying your shoelaces. In fact, it is so poor that you often trip on your shoelaces. Second, let us assume that you have come to counseling to deal with this self-defeating behavior. Third, let us postulate that you first want to know "why" you have this problem with your shoelaces. Now, as your counselor my first task would be to teach you a few lessons.
    LESSON ONE Even if we find out "why" you tie your shoelaces poorly, that will not change how you tie your shoelaces. Even if we find out that it was your mother, father, sister, brother, cousin, aunt, uncle, grandmother, grandfather, teacher, coach, maid, nurse, baby-sitter, etc., who taught you to tie your shoelaces so poorly--that will not change how you tie your shoelaces. Even if we remember the very first time you learned to tie your shoelaces wrongly, that will not change how you tie your shoelaces. Even if you label all your feelings about tying your shoes, cry about tying your shoes, express feelings for hours about tying your shoes, get mad at people who taught you wrong, explore the deep meaning of tying your shoes, work out your conflicts about your parents, record and analyze your dreams, free associate, relive the first time, have a rebirthing experience, role-play responding to your teachers, learn new social skills, visualize your standing up to your trainers in the past, talk to different parts of yourself in therapy about how hard it all was, are reparented, have past life therapy, engage in dramas about

tying your shoes, write endless journal notes about tying your shoes, explore your script issues, restructure your family, change your diet, get detoxed, move, change jobs, stop eating sugar, get divorced, have body work, have body massages, have an emotional enema, write letters, beat pillows, scream, reframe, rewrite your life story, get your chi rebalanced, tap different parts of your body, move your eyes left and right, or whatever current technique is fashionable--it will not be tying your shoes in a new more effective way. We do not need to know "why" in order to know "how" you are doing what you are doing. For instance, no one really knows "why" electricity works. But since we know "how" it works, we can make use of electricity. Even after we know exactly how you are tying your shoelaces that will not change how you are tying your shoelaces.

LESSON TWO Tying your shoelaces the way you are tying them now feels "natural" and "normal" because it is a habit--not because it is natural or normal. Learning to tie your shoelaces a new way--no matter how much better or how perfect a way it is--will be uncomfortable and will take persistent practice and work. The new more effective way of tying your shoelaces will feel "unnatural" and "abnormal" not because it is wrong--but only because it is against your current habit.

LESSON THREE You have two jobs.

1) Unlearn the old ineffective way of tying your shoelaces; 2) Learn a new more effective way of tying your shoelaces. This makes it harder but that does not mean impossible. It only means that it is more work and will take more time than just learning from scratch. Unlearning is harder than learning. This is why many companies prefer to hire people who are not trained so that they can train them their way without having to fight or argue with their old training.

LESSON FOUR

The only way you will switch the way that you are tying your shoelaces to a more productive way is--through persistent practice. You have to think, feel, and act against the old way until the new way becomes your new habit. Thinking and insight alone will not do it. Feeling and talking alone will not do it. Trying and procrastinating will not do it. You must **recognize** the wrong way and the right way, you must remove the wrong way by deciding to give it up, and you must **replace** the old way with the new way. Recognizing involves thinking and insight. Removing involves feeling and motivation. Replacing involves doing and habit. So you need to think, feel, and act against the old to make the new natural.

Now, let us begin to help you to recognize the poor way, to recognize a better way, to feel strongly enough to switch ways, and to learn how to practice the right way. AN **ANSWER** Answers to "why" vary according to the preferences of the hunters as to which target to blame. Targets can be grouped into being either of an inner or an outer nature. Inner targets can be grouped either as responsibility or spirituality issues. Outer targets can be grouped either as physical or social environment issues. Hence, there are many permutations, many possible combinations of causes and so many possible explanations.

One answer that makes sense and can help has 3 parts:

(1) You are biologically prone to the negative;

(2) You are sociologically conditioned to the negative;

(3) You are habitually drawn to the negative. Bottom line: work against your negative tendencies whether they are natural, social, or just a bad habit.

The Rules For Being Human

You will receive a body. You may like it or hate it, but it will be yours for the entire period this time around. • You will learn lessons. You are enrolled in a full-time, informal school called life. Each day in this school you will have the opportunity to learn lessons. You may like the lessons or think them irrelevant and stupid. • There are no mistakes, only lessons. Growth is a process of trial and error, experimentation. The "failed" experiments are as much a part of the process as the experiment that ultimately "works". • A lesson is repeated until it is learned. A lesson will be presented to you in various forms until you have learned it, then you can go on to the next lesson. • Learning lessons does not end. There is no part of life that does not contain its lessons. If you are alive, there are lessons to be learned. • There" is no better than "here". When your "there" has become a "here", you will simply obtain another "there" that will, again, look better than "here". • Others are merely mirrors of you. You cannot love or hate something about another person unless it reflects to you something you love or hate about yourself. • "What you make of your life is up to you. You have all the tools and resources you need; what you do with them is up to you. The choice is yours. • The answers lie inside you. The answers to life's questions lie inside you. All you need to do is look, listen and trust. • You Will Forget All of This (Some of the Time).

Universality: Way of Peace

One of the most important principles for all time is: universality. Universality is the understanding that there is **only one human nature.** Human nature is universal, is the same for all humans. "And hath made of one blood all nations of men for to dwell on all the face of the earth, and hath determined the times before appointed, and the bounds of their habitation;"-Acts 17:26

"For who maketh thee to differ from another? and what hast thou that thou didst not receive? now if thou didst receive it, why dost thou glory, as if thou hadst not received it?"--I Corinthians 4:7 "Wherefore putting away lying, speak every man truth with his neighbour: for we are members one of another. "--Ephesians 4:25 **Without the principle of universality there is no real forgiveness.** "Thou shalt not avenge, nor bear any grudge against the children of thy people, but thou shalt love thy neighbour as thyself: I am the LORD."--Leviticus 19:18 **Without the principle of universality there is no chance to end racism, ethnic hatred, and genocide. Universality and pride cannot coexist.** "1 charge thee before God, and the Lord Jesus Christ, and the elect angels, that thou observe these things without preferring one before another, doing nothing by partiality."-I Timothy 5:21

"Therefore as by the offence of one judgment came upon all men to condemnation; even so by the righteousness of one the free gift came upon all men unto justification of life."-Romans 5:18 **The *greatest* enemy of the principle of universality is the thinking style known as self-esteem.**

"But the wisdom that is from above is first pure, then peaceable, gentle, and easy to be intreated, full of mercy and good fruits, without partiality, and without hypocrisy."-James 3:17 "There is neither Jew nor Greek, there is neither bond nor free, there is neither male nor female: for ye are all one in Christ Jesus."--Galatians 3:28

"Where there is neither Greek nor Jew, circumcision nor uncircumcision, Barbarian, Scythian, bond nor free: but Christ is all, and in all."--Colossians 3:11 "What then? are we better than they? No, in no wise: for we have before proved both Jews and Gentiles, that they are all under sin;"--Romans 3:9

"One who you think should be hit is none else but you. One who you think should be governed is none else but you. One who you think should be tortured is none else but you. One who you think should be enslaved is none else but you. One who you think should be killed is none else but you. A sage is ingenuous and leads his life after comprehending the parity of the killed and the killer. Therefore, neither does he cause violence to others nor does he make others do so."--Jainism, Acarangasutra 5:101-2

"And the second is like unto it, Thou shalt love thy neighbour as thyself,"--Matthew 22:39

"Then Peter opened his mouth, and said, Of a truth I perceive that God is no respecter of persons: But in every nation he that feareth him, and worketh righteousness, is accepted with him."--Acts 10:34-35

Goals of universality is the nonhierarchical relating of persons.

"For there is no respect of persons with God."--Romans 2:11

The Rules for Being Human • You will receive a body. You may like it or hate it, but It will be yours for the entire period this time around. • You will learn lessons. You are enrolled in a full-time, informal school called life. Each day in this school you will have the opportunity to learn lessons. You may like the lessons or think them irrelevant and stupid. • There are no mistakes, only lessons. Growth is a process of trial and error, experimentation. The "failed" experiments are as much a part of the process as the experiment that ultimately "works". • A lesson Is repeated until it is learned. A lesson will be presented to you in various forms until you have learned It, then you can go on to the next lesson. • Learning lessons does not end. There is no part of life that does not contain its lessons. If you are alive, there are lessons to be learned. • There" is no better than "here". When your "there" has become a "here", you will simply obtain another "there" that will, again, look better than "here". • Others are merely mirrors of you. You cannot love or hate something about another person unless it reflects to you something you love or hate about yourself. • "What you make of your life is up to you. You have all the tools and resources you need; what you do with them is up to you. The choice is yours. • The answers lie inside you. The answers to life's questions lie inside you. All you need to do is look, listen and trust. • You Will Forget All of This (Some of the Time).

50 Short Disputes I. Prove right now that you are the behavior you are judging yourself to be! Where is the evidence that you are the behavior that you are judging yourself to be? 2. Where is it written that people are or can become their behavior? Where is it written that your being becomes your mistakes? 3. Whose law is it that you must regard yourself as your behavior, and especially so if it is negative? Where is the evidence that you must become your negative behavior? 4. Prove that because you did some ignorant or foolish thing in the past that that damns you to forever repeat it. Where is the evidence that just because you behaved badly that that makes you, your being, bad? 5. Prove that the behavior is the judgment of it! Where is the evidence that the behavior and the judgment about it are one and the same? 6. Is a car its actions? How can you be your actions? You are much more than a car! Is the air its actions? You are more than air! 7. Where is the proof that you are definitions? Aren't you your nonverbal being? 8. Prove that your being can become some thing? What happens to yourself when you imagine **it** becomes things, thoughts9 9. Why can't you ever find and demonstrate yourself as definitions, behaviors, labels, words, thoughts, images, concepts, etc., in the here-and-now? Why can they only occur about the past? Isn't all thought only of the past? Aren't you in the present!? 10. What are the fair, just, and consistent procedures that you use to judge yourself to be one thought and not another? Is there any way to validate why some of your thoughts should get the "I" label and some shouldn't? 11. Prove that your unique being is general just because you need it to be to assume it is thoughts, labels, descriptions, etc., because their nature is general. 12. Prove that you were ever able to surround and-or experience your entire self at once so that you could know it to rate or judge it as anything. - 13. Prove that you were able to stop time and your own flowing, your own process so that you could judge yourself to be some static thought? When did you capture yourself? 14. Show how you can now be your past behaviors when they are obviously not here, but are only represented by distorted and incomplete memories.

15. Prove that thought is your experience of yourself. What happened to your sensations of yourself without thought? What are the thoughts about if they are you and you have thoughts about yourself? 16. Where is the evidence that thought knows reality, knows all of it, knows enough truth to make any judgments? When does thought perceive or sense under its own power? 17. Prove that your thoughts are the experiences that they claim you were and are. Can thoughts be experiences or only limited, partial, and fragmented representations of them? If thoughts are not the real experiences, then what are you if you are thoughts? 18. Prove those thoughts, definitions, descriptions, behaviors, sensations, perceptions, or whatever--can know your being and your infinitely complex situation. Don't they always have to isolate you from your situation in order to classify' you?

Can or have you ever existed independently of your situation, environment, milieu, circumstances, and conditions? 19. If yourself is thoughts, definitions, descriptions, behaviors, images, etc., then how does it continue, how does it remain alive, how is it more than a rock or a robot? 20. Prove that thought is or can be responsible for yourselfhood or your behavior. 21. Where is the evidence that static thoughts can ever know or understand the dynamic self? 22. Where is the evidence that static thoughts have ever or can ever be your dynamic self? 23. Where is the evidence that static thoughts are ever or can ever do your dynamic self? 24. Aren't all your thoughts of self at best only maps of the territoiy of the self? Is the map the territory? Can it be? Should it be mistaken for or treated as such? 25. Prove that the necessarily limited bits of reality that thoughts, descriptions, and definitions are--can be about or can be your whole self. Realize that even a true sum of the parts can't be the whole, let alone the sum of your limited definitions. 26. Where is the proof that your judgments of yourself are more accurate or more real than anyone else's of yourself? How do or can you determine whose judgments are accurate? Yours are too subjective and theirs are too lacking in your experience. So which judgments are supposed to be you--yours or theirs? 27. Can thought observe the self? If thought cannot observe the self, then how can thought know the self? If thought cannot know the self, then how can thought claim to represent the self? If thought cannot even represent the self, then how can thought claim to be the self? 28. Can the observer observe itself? Can yourself observe itself? Who is it that observes the self and names the self as something other than that which is observing it?

29. Does the self see the self? Does the self name the self? If the self is naming itself, then how can the self be the name of itself? 30. Prove that you can be words when words have

variable meanings and are not limited to any one interpretation. Won't everyone interpret your words differently? So which of the different interpretations are you? Prove yours are more real, accurate, knowing, or complete than everyone else's. 31. Prove that you are in the present what you thought you were in the past just because you thought you were before. How does that follow logically? Isn't that a non sequitur? 32. Since nothing, including you, can ever repeat, then how is it that you believe that you are something that has already occurred in the past? Are you what has happened that cannot happen again? Isn't this just what you claim when you claim you are what you did!? 33. How can you repeat being the thought that you thought you were when you thought you were that thought in the past? 34. Where is the evidence that the nonverbal self, the true self, can ever be known or captured by any verbal means? *35.* Prove that your ego is permanent. Isn't it your assumption that your ego is permanent when you define and create it using concrete and static thoughts and memories of experiences? Are not all human experiences fleeting? Isn't it true that anything observable is impermanent? How can you make yourself into what is no more? 36. Prove that you are one with your ego, with yourself-concepts, with yourself as thoughts. Aren't you separate? Don't you judge, choose, persecute, repress, praise, enjoy, suffer, and experience all manner of sensations in regard to thought? Aren't you in the present and thoughts in the past sometimes; aren't you in the present observing thoughts in the present sometimes; aren't you in the present imagining thoughts in the future sometimes? When do the two meet and form you? 37. Where is the evidence that your relationship with the world is a knowledge-thing? Is this not what you claim when you think of yourself in relation to your experiences as something, as some judgment!? 38. Where is the evidence that your knowledge-thing of self is part of your knowledge- thing of your relationship with the world? That is, how does yourself-image become reborn as your social-image? 39. Does yourself exist in two separate worlds? Does yourself exist in the world of self images and also in the world of social-images? Can yourself exist in both of these worlds at the same time? What happens to yourself when these worlds collide? 40. Where is the evidence that your knowledge-thing of the other person is a part of your knowledge-thing of your relationship with them? That is, how does yourself-image for another fit into and become a part of your social-image for them? Does this transform their self?

41. Where is the proof that yourself is the separation, the individuation of your knowledge-thing of yourself from your knowledge-thing of your relationship with the world? In other words, by what logic do you claim that you are more yourself-images than you are your social-images? 42. Prove the reality of any knowledge-things--enmeshed or differentiated? That is, are knowledge-things (e.g., self-images) anything more than imagination, than imagined realties that have no substance, form, or direct relation to a self existing in the real world (outside of the mind)? 43. Prove the reality of the imagined relationships of knowledge-things? That is, is the relating of knowledge-things (e.g., social-images) any more than imagination? Your social-images are an imagined reality that has no substance, form, or direct correlation in the real world (outside of the human mind): Maya. 44. Where is the evidence that you are a god who can create themselves out of thoughts, definitions, and descriptions? Isn't self-esteem just fanciful thinking!? *45.* Prove that you are omniscient and omnipresent. Prove that your senses are omni directional. Obviously you can't. Hence, all your judgments, observations, knowings, and claims are limited and at best only arbitrary. If

they are limited, then yourself is limited by them. If yourself is limited by them, then what happens to the parts of self that are left out of your definitions? If they are limited, then how can they honestly be the full you? 46. Please show us your logical system for determining your ego. What? You have none! You mean to say that if you are honest then you must admit that you determine what yourself is without rhyme or reason? Then how can the self you fabricate be fair, honest, or real? 47. When did you study and learn a system of self-esteem thinking that would at least more often that not provide an irate picture of you? You mean to say that you decide who and what you are without anything more than emotion and whim to guide you? Then surely you cannot take the resulting nonsense seriously! 48. Do you magically become whatever it is you think you are? Do others also magically become the thoughts that you think they are? 49. I suppose it is not superstitious to think that if someone does not like you that you have become some bad thing. I suppose it is not superstitious to think that if you are having a bad day that it is because you are a bad thing. I suppose it is not superstitious to think that if you have something bad that that makes you a bad thing. I suppose you wouldn't mind if I left this planet!? *50.* When do all the definitions of a university become that university? That is, if we collect all of the definitions of anything and put them into one place, will we then have that thing? No. Yet, you do not bother to collect all of the definitions of yourself into one place. No. You can take any one definition and claim that it is you whenever you feel like it. Great job. Yes, humans are quite rational. Please, let me out of here now!

A Parable on Responsibility   You are stuck in a deep dark hole. Above you, you can see different kinds of people walking by. You shout up to them and they wave and walk by. You get angry and start to blame and damn them for your being stuck in the hole. They still just wave and walk by. Determined, you start to yell at them and to damn them even more virulently. Some now stop to listen. One agrees with you and says that he will go and write a law against people being in holes and leaves. Another lowers down some water and commiserates with you but does nothing to get you out. Still another starts yelling along with you at others as they pass by Of all the reactions you get, none helps you to get out of the hole. You start to think that there must be something wrong with you. You now start to damn yourself for being in the hole. However, this form of damning doesn't help you get out either. But you are at least persistent and now continue to damn those above and yourself as well. Yet, despite all your best efforts, you remain in the hole. One day an old man with a long white beard stops by your hole. Waiting for a break in your whining, he finally asks "Can you stand to know the truth?" You reply that since you can stand being in the hole, you can stand anything. The old man replies, "Then I will tell you the only way out of your hole." "First, you are right to hold others as responsible for your being in the hole, though certainly not all who pass by. Others not only dug your hole for you, they also threw you in it. And far worse, they taught you to damn whoever is responsible." "Why shouldn't I danm them? Why shouldn't I complain? You even agree that they put me here to begin with!" "Because that is the hole. It does **not matter if you are damning them or yourself— that is the hole.** Yes, they are responsible for digging the hole in the first place. Yes, they are responsible for throwing you in the hole in the first place. But only you are or can be responsible for your staying in the hole right now." "How can that be? Why don't you just lift me out?" "Because you would fall back in as soon as you started to damn those who threw you in the first time." "But if they are responsible then why shouldn't I damn them." "This is the key to your getting out and staying out of the hole: responsibility does NOT **equal or excuse damning.** It doesn't matter if you damn them or yourself--either one will recreate the hole around you!" "It sounds like you want me to be responsible for my own problems when you admit that they did do me wrong. How can that work?"

"They are responsible *for* putting you there in the first place as they raised, educated, and trained you for the hole. But only you are responsible as an adult for staying there." "How can I be responsible and they be responsible and no one gets any blame?" "Responsibility or accountability are NOT the same as damning. **Once you can see them** as **responsible** without damning them, and yourself as responsible without damning yourself, then and only then will you live outside the hole." "What you say just doesn't feel right." "The hole is a wonderful trap that becomes a habit, and whatever you practice a lot feels right. You are in the hole if you damn them and you are in the hole if you damn yourself. So you feel like you are trapped. But the trap is only in your mind. Separate responsibility from damning. Practice total acceptance of self and others with mistakes and wrongs." "I just don't get it." "Let me try once more. Not only did ,they dig your hole and throw you in your hole, they made it certain that you would never get out of your hole. They made you your own prisoner by teaching you that if you do bad you are bad and if you are responsible for bad then you are bad. Now, you won't face your own responsibility for staying in the hole because that supposedly makes you bad according to your inherited logic. As a result, you now keep yourself in the hole NOT them-- they don't have to" "That Just sounds like you want to blame me" "You just proved my point. Quite an ingenious trap isn't it? Let your mind work on what I said. I have to go now. Good luck sorting it out." **MORAL OF THE STORY** The moral of the story is that responsibility without damning self or others is freedom and responsibility with self-damning and-or other-damning is the prison, the hole.

PROBLEMS The problem is that others are responsible for leading you astray. So you feel self- righteous and damn them. And so dig the hole for yourself The problem is also that you think you are responsible as you must be stupid, defective, or somehow inferior. Again, you dig the hole by damning. The problem is also that since responsibility equals damning for you, you cannot face your responsibility to dig yourself out of the hole as it is too painful, it is only more of the hole for you. The problem is that no matter which way you turn the issue of responsibility, it will only lead to the hole of damning for you. The problem is that you would rather damn them than damn yourself as for you it is either-or: someone must be damned so it might as well be them. The problem is damning will never be peace, love, understanding, forgiveness, happiness, freedom, play,

Do the Absolute-Right Thing Anyway "The time is always right to do what is right."--Martin Luther King, Jr. 1. Forget all other options and do the right thing anyway. 2. Forget getting even and do the right thing anyway. 3. Forget how the weather or your mother acted and do the right thing anyway. 4. Forget that no one will ever know and do the right thing anyway. 5. Forget that you deserve it and do the right thing anyway. 6. Forget their hurt feelings and do the right thing anyway. 7. Forget their wrongs and do the right thing anyway. 8. Forget what they do or don't do and you do the right thing anyway. 9. Forget what you did or didn't do and now do the right thing anyway. 10. Forget your challenges, pressures, and obstacles and do the right thing anyway. 11. Forget your conditioning, training, and upbringing and do the right thing anyway. 12. Forget your conflicts and do the right thing anyway. 13. Forget your desire for sympathy and do the right thing anyway. 14. Forget your desire to get rescued and do the right thing anyway. 15. Forget your discomforts and do the right thing anyway. 16. Forget your excuses and do the right thing anyway. 17. Forget your experiences of prejudice, hate, and injustice and do the right thing anyway. 18. Forget your habit of emotional blackmail and do the right thing anyway. 19. Forget your hate and do the right thing anyway. 20. Forget your hurt feelings and do the right thing anyway. 21. Forget your identification with the problem and do the right thing anyway. 22. Forget your joy in demanding and do the right thing anyway. 23. Forget your loss of fame or fortune and do the right thing anyway. 24. Forget your loss of friends and do the right thing anyway. 25. Forget your loss of popularity or friends and do the right thing anyway. 26. Forget your lust for drama and do the right thing anyway. 27. Forget your lust for money and do the right thing anyway. 28. Forget your lust for pride and do the right thing anyway. 29. Forget your need for success and do the right thing anyway. 30. Forget your need to please people and do the right thing anyway. 31. Forget your rationalizations and do the right thing anyway. 32. Forget your reasons to act lazily and do the right thing anyway. 33. Forget your revenge and do the right thing anyway. 34. Forget your sense of self as the problem and do the right thing anyway. 35. Forget your suffering, hurt, pain, abuse and do the right thing anyway. 36. Forget your trials, tribulations, and hardships and do the right thing anyway. 37. Forget your wanting power over others and do the right thing anyway. 38. Forget jour wanting to manipulate others and do the right thing anyway. 39 Forget your wants and do the right thing anyway 40 Forget your whining, blaming, and damning and do the right thing anyway 41 Forget your wrongs and do the right thing anyway

The problem is you must be responsible for your responses and you cannot be for you are damned if you are and damned if you aren't.

TRAP OF TRAPS — The worst trap of this trap is that you now want to dig holes for others as your way of getting out of your hole! You have become them! "No one can rescue you but you." Please note; "forget" in the above list means to: NOT keep in mind, NOT dwell on, NOT think about all day. "Forget" in the above list does NOT mean to: not remember, never remember, erase from memory, deny consequences, not learn from experience, not acknowledge a danger or hazard. 1. Do the right thing and people will accuse you of doing the wrong thing. Do the right thing anyway. 2. People may never forgive you for helping them. Do the right thing for them anyway. 3. People will damn you for failing and succeeding. Do the right thing by struggling to succeed anyway. 4. People will damn you no matter what you do. Do the right thing anyway. **5.** People will do the wrong thing to you. Do the right thing for them anyway. 6. People will doubt your best dreams. Do the right thing and dream anyway. 7. People will forget your help and claim they helped themselves. Do the right thing and help them anyway. 8. People will misunderstand your intentions and motives. Do the right thing anyway. 9. People will steal your ideas and take credit for your work. Do the right thing and contribute anyway.

<u>Whining, Blaming, & Damning Prevent Solutions</u> "He therefore that despiseth despiseth not man, but God, who hath also given unto us His holy Spirit."--I Thessalonians 4:8 The three big hindrances to problem-solving and coping are whining, blaming, and damning. Whining, blaming, and damning show that you are putting ego pleasure ahead of relationships. Whining, blaming, and damning show that your priority is self-righteousness. Whining, blaming, and damning show that you are willing to sacrifice yourself and others for the pride of knowing better. Whining, blaming, and damning are when you hypocritically collect and send out the negative while being mad at others for doing the same. Whining, blaming, and damning are when you do evil in the name of good. Whining, blaming, and damning are when you serve the negative under the pretext of the good. Whining, blaming, and damning are when you cover, your service to the negative with the positive. Whining, blaming, and damning are the favorite strongholds of those with a victim mentality. Whining, blaming, and damning are the payoffs of codependents. Whining, blaming, and damning maintain the cycle of abuse. Whining, blaming, and damning are part of the drama game of abuse. Whining is abuse as whining promotes and incorporates damning. Blaming is abuse as it is depowering by keeping you externally referenced. When you are externally referented you try to control others instead of self, and so are out of control or without your personal power.

Damning is abuse as damning objectifies and dehumanizes. Objectifying is the prerequisite to genocide. Damning occurs at every stage of the cycle of abuse. Without damning there can be no abuse. The roles in the cycle, of abuse are: judge, prosecutor, offender, victim, defender, and jailer. Danming is what all the roles have in common.

<u>Anger Notes</u>

<u>Depression Notes</u>

<u>Anxiety Notes</u>

Stress Notes

_____

_____

_____

_____

_____

_____

_____

_____

_____

_____

_____

_____

_____

_____

<u>Self Notes</u>

<u>Affirmation Notes</u>

<u>Recap Notes</u>

Would you like to see your manuscript become a book?

If you are interested in becoming a PublishAmerica author, please submit your manuscript for possible publication to us at:

mybook@publishamerica.com

You may also mail in your manuscript to:

PublishAmerica
PO Box 151
Frederick, MD 21705

www.publishamerica.com

CPSIA information can be obtained
at www.ICGtesting.com
Printed in the USA
FSOW02n1253261016
26613FS